THIRD EDITION

Writing the
WINNING
Thesis or
Dissertation

THIRD EDITION

Writing the
WINNING
Thesis or Dissertation

A STEP-BY-STEP GUIDE

Randy L. Joyner
William A. Rouse
Allan A. Glatthorn

CORWIN
A SAGE Company

CORWIN
A SAGE Company

FOR INFORMATION:

Corwin
A SAGE Company
2455 Teller Road
Thousand Oaks, California 91320
(800) 233-9936
www.corwin.com

SAGE Publications Ltd.
1 Oliver's Yard
55 City Road
London EC1Y 1SP
United Kingdom

SAGE Publications India Pvt. Ltd.
B 1/I 1 Mohan Cooperative Industrial Area
Mathura Road, New Delhi 110 044
India

SAGE Publications Asia-Pacific Pte. Ltd.
3 Church Street
#10-04 Samsung Hub
Singapore 049483

Acquisitions Editor: Arnis Burvikovs
Associate Editor: Desirée A. Bartlett
Editorial Assistant: Kimberly Greenberg
Production Editors: Cassandra Margaret Seibel,
                                        Amy Schroller
Copy Editor: Deanna Noga
Typesetter: C&M Digitals (P) Ltd.
Proofreader: Scott Oney
Indexer: Maria Sosnowski
Cover Designer: Michael Dubowe
Permissions Editor: Karen Ehrmann

Copyright © 2013 by Corwin

Printed in the United States of America.

Library of Congress Cataloging-in-Publication Data

Joyner, Randy L.

Writing the winning thesis or dissertation : a step-by-step guide / Randy L. Joyner, William A. Rouse, Allan A. Glatthorn.—3rd ed.

p. cm.
Includes bibliographical references and index.
Prev. ed. main entry under Glatthorn, Allan A.

ISBN 978-1-4522-5878-2 (pbk.)

1. Dissertations, Academic. 2. Report writing. 3. Research. I. Rouse, William A. II. Glatthorn, Allan A., 1924- III. Glatthorn, Allan A., 1924- Writing the winning dissertation. IV. Title.

LB2369.G56 2013
808.06'6378—dc23   2012024496

This book is printed on acid-free paper.

12 13 14 15 16 10 9 8 7 6 5 4 3 2 1

Contents

Preface

The undertaking of an advanced degree program that requires the writing of a thesis or a dissertation is a mighty task. Furthermore, graduate students who enter such a degree program are investing many hours in research and writing as well as sacrificing personal family time to complete the degree program. According to Allan Glatthorn (1924–2007)—the author of the first edition of *Writing the Winning Thesis or Dissertation: A Step-by-Step Guide*, and another East Carolina University colleague, H. C. Hudgins, Jr., a good, winning dissertation is a done dissertation. Allan directed many dissertations during his career; his guidance and influence assisted many advanced-degree students and colleagues in writing a winning dissertation. Allan's previous research, writings, and mentorship had a profound impact on the two principal authors of the third edition. The wisdom shared by Allan in the first edition was the basis for the second and third editions; many of his remarks are still valid five years after his death. Allan's wisdom and guidance in the dissertating process has been and continues to be greatly missed.

After directing and serving as committee members for many dissertations, it was time to share more systematically what the authors had learned from that experience. Furthermore, the authors decided to create a book that would demystify the writing of theses and dissertations, so that advanced degree students would no longer be terrified when preparing to write and actually writing these scholarly works. This book resulted.

It is an experience-based, practical work that takes you through the process one step at a time.

The emphasis here is on a winning, completed dissertation. We, the authors, do not want to discuss the writing of a "quickie" dissertation, of which you will be ashamed as you continue in your career. We are concerned with providing guidance to produce a quality study that will reflect well on you and help you advance in your career. As mentioned earlier, you—the advanced-degree student—will be investing considerable time, energy, and money in this endeavor; you want the return to reflect that significant investment.

Throughout the book, for the sake of simplicity, the authors ordinarily use the term *dissertation* to mean both the master's thesis and the doctoral dissertation, noting any distinctions when appropriate and important. For the most part, the processes for writing both the thesis and the dissertation are similar, with the exception of scope and complexity.

This newly revised and updated third edition begins in a familiar place: the important foundation steps—from laying the foundations for the dissertation to holding a preproposal conference. While some educators want to rush through these preliminary steps, the early steps represent a systematic way of planning carefully and laying a solid foundation.

Based on comments from the users of previous editions, two chapters in the second edition were eliminated, but the relevant content from those two chapters was incorporated into other chapters. As the role of technology in the educational process is constantly changing, each chapter contains a "Technology Technique," with the authors' intent being to assist the user with the way or ways in which technology may be used to facilitate the dissertating process. Furthermore, a new chapter, Chapter 2, was added to discuss the role of the institution granting the degree and that institution's requirements for satisfying the degree requirements. While Chapter 2 has been designed to be useful for all advanced-degree students, each institution and each chair have their own special requirements. Close and continuing contact with your dissertation chair is essential. In those cases where the chair's advice differs from ours, follow the recommendations of your chair.

A final comment by the authors: An important underlying component of completing a winning dissertation is communication. Through the years, the authors have seen advanced-degree students complete the doctoral degree coursework. Yet after the completion of the coursework, many advanced-degree students are never seen again. When a dissertation chair attempts to contact the students, the students do not respond. It is imperative that advanced-degree-seeking students maintain contact with the dissertation chair; the role of and need for continued communication between dissertation director and student is emphasized throughout the book.

In many ways, this book represents a collaborative effort. Our chief debt is to all those educators with whom the authors have worked and from whom we have learned. The authors feel most indebted to all the doctoral students whom we have advised. Like most teachers, the authors teach because for us it is the best way to learn, and without the professional staff at Corwin, the third edition would not have been a reality. And as all writers of theses and dissertations know, there were behind the scenes our supportive and caring families, cheering us on and tolerating our absorption with the task of producing a winning, completed book.

Randy L. Joyner
William A. Rouse, Jr.

About the Authors

Randy L. Joyner is an adjunct professor in the Department of Curriculum and Instruction in the College of Education, Appalachian State University, Boone, NC. He is retired from the Department of Educational Leadership in the College of Education of East Carolina University, where he directed or served as committee member for 25 dissertations. Furthermore, he has served as a doctoral committee member at Virginia Polytechnic Institute and State University, Blacksburg; and North Carolina State University, Raleigh. He has received several awards for his research: the Delta Pi Epsilon doctoral research award, the Omicron Tau Theta Iota Chapter Research Award, and the Delta Pi Epsilon Alpha Chapter Research Award. The results of his research have been published in national and international journals.

William A. Rouse Jr. is an Associate Professor in the Department of Educational Leadership in the College of Education, East Carolina University, Greenville, NC. He was a public school teacher and a secondary school principal prior to joining the faculty at East Carolina University. He has worked with several school districts' administrators to refocus their efforts on effective school leadership practices that result in a dynamic teaching and learning environment. He has also worked with a school district to redesign large comprehensive high schools into smaller learning communities resulting in increased student academic performance. In 2004, he coauthored the Outstanding Paper delivered at the Delta Pi Epsilon National Research Conference; his research has been published in national refereed journals.

Allan A. Glatthorn (1924–2007) was a major contributor to the third edition; his research used in the preparation of the first and second editions of *Writing the Winning Thesis or Dissertation: A Step-by-Step Guide* was the foundation for the third edition. He was the Distinguished Research Professor of Education (Emeritus) in the College of Education of East Carolina University, where he advised doctoral students, chaired dissertations, and taught courses in supervision and curriculum. He was formerly Professor of Education at the Graduate School of Education of the University of Pennsylvania. Prior to his university assignments, he was a high school teacher and principal. In his work as a professor, he chaired close to 100 dissertations. He is the author of numerous professional books, several of which have been published by Corwin.

I

Establishing the Foundations

Laying the Groundwork for the Thesis and Dissertation

You have reached an important stage in your career, preparing to write a thesis or dissertation—a stage where many graduate students flounder. In 1997, D'Andrea reported that lack of structure in the dissertation process may be a key element in the failure of many students to complete their program. Yet in 2012 the lack of structure in the dissertation process continues to be a major obstacle in the completion of the dissertation (CPED, 2012; National Council of Professors of Educational Administration, 2011; Northern Illinois University Counseling, 2012).This book is designed to provide you with the structure you need to write a winning dissertation, which is a "done dissertation."

Writing a winning dissertation begins with establishing a solid foundation. This chapter will help you establish such a foundation by understanding the special nature of the dissertation, and by making some preliminary decisions. As explained in the preface, the term *dissertation* is generally used throughout the work to refer to both master's theses and doctoral dissertations. Since there are some differences, however, it seems appropriate to include in this introductory chapter an explanation of some crucial differences between the thesis and the dissertation.

Occasionally problems, both personal and professional, may develop for the student that may affect the "dissertating" process. To help you, *a dissertating student*, deal with such issues, this chapter will also assist in clarifying the roles of the committee and its dynamics. Furthermore, the chapter addresses how you might prevent and deal with some of the most common problems.

UNDERSTANDING THE SPECIAL NATURE OF THE DISSERTATION

Like most writing, the dissertation is written to accomplish certain purposes with a specific audience—and its unique nature is perhaps best understood by analyzing purpose and audience.

Purposes in Writing the Dissertation

Purpose is perhaps best understood by examining it from three perspectives: institutional purpose, personal purpose, and communication purpose. The institutional purpose is to ensure that the degree holder has made a contribution to the field as well as to uphold an honored academic tradition. The dissertation has an ancient history, because it originates at the medieval university where it was required of all those who wanted to teach. The dissertation now, of course, is perceived by university faculty as a demonstration of the candidate's fitness to conduct and publish research, and to enter their scholarly ranks. The faculty also requires the dissertation because they take seriously the mission of generating and disseminating new knowledge. Furthermore, the dissertation is simply a widely accepted form for such dissemination.

You probably have several personal purposes in undertaking the dissertation. The foremost, obviously, is to earn the degree. However, you should view the dissertation as something more than an unpleasant requirement—what some students disparagingly call "the fee for the union card" or "the right of passage." You should see it also as a way of learning. In the struggle to write the dissertation, you will learn much about yourself and about the topic you have researched. Writing is a way of knowing and thinking: The process of systematizing knowledge and finding a form to express that knowledge becomes a means of discovering meaning, or as several writers have put it, "I don't know what I know until I try to write it." Such learning will foster your personal and professional growth.

Your dissertation will be a better one if you take seriously the expectation that you will make a contribution to scholarly knowledge. Even though few dissertations report earth-shaking discoveries, the good ones add incrementally to the body of professional knowledge. Winning or completed dissertations extend knowledge, even if the topic has often been studied. Suppose, for example, that a dissertation reports research indicating that end-of-course testing was not an effective measure of student academic performance. That finding does not negate all the previous studies that found end-of-course testing to be an effective measure of student academic performance; it simply says to future researchers that the issue requires additional study.

The communicative purpose is clear and simple: You write to report the results of research. You do not write to persuade, to entertain, or to express personal feelings—but to inform. That informing function indicates that the primary quality of the writing is clarity, not creativity.

All these purposes—the institutional, the personal, and the communicative—interact to shape the dissertation in a special way.

The Audiences for the Dissertation

Your audiences are also several. You write for yourself, of course, and you must be satisfied with what you have written. When you have finished the dissertation, you should feel a sense of pride in what you have accomplished.

You write for your committee, and their predilections, preferences, and idiosyncrasies must be recognized and addressed. In a way, they are the most important audience, since they will scrutinize your dissertation most carefully. Although others may give it only a cursory look, the committee will examine it page by page.

You write for the faculty as a whole, and institutional standards must be met. The faculty will award you the degree, and the requirements they have set for the dissertation's form and content should be respected, even if they may seem unreasonable to you.

Finally, of course, you write for other members of your profession. Your dissertation will become a small part of a complex information network; your findings and conclusions will be read by other doctoral students and researchers in the field.

Analyze the Special Characteristics of the Dissertation

What results, then, from this intersection of purposes and audiences is a special type of writing. The dissertation is a report of research intended primarily for a scholarly audience. It is *not* a longer version of a term paper. It is *not* an anecdotal account of your professional success. And it is *not* a personal statement of your philosophy or a collection of your opinions. It is an objective, documented, and detailed report of your research.

Although the specific requirements for the dissertation will vary from department to department and school to school, it is possible to identify certain general characteristics that derive from this analysis of purpose and audience.

First, dissertations are long—longer than a term paper, shorter than a book. The average length of dissertations seems to be approximately 200 pages, usually ranging between 125 and 225 pages. Those are only general guidelines, of course. There are differences in fields of study: Dissertations in the natural sciences tend to be shorter than those in the social sciences. There are differences in methodology: Dissertations reporting ethnographic investigations tend to be longer than those reporting experimental studies. The practical advice here is simply to write the dissertation so that it is long enough to tell your story without boring your committee.

Second, dissertations look scholarly—they contain citations of previous research. Your dissertation is expected to build upon previous knowledge, and as an inexperienced research scholar you are expected to know the literature and be able to cite it appropriately. You can't simply make assertions; you must document them. The journalist writes, "The skills and duties required of a superintendent today differ greatly from those required over 100 years ago." The scholar writes, "According to several recent studies (Boldt, 2004; Candoli, 1995; Cuban, 1976; Kowalski, 1999) many practicing superintendents agree that the superintendent position has gone through fundamental changes since the first school superintendent was appointed in 1837."

Third, dissertations sound scholarly. While there seems to be a trend away from the highly formal style and a reaction against turgid academic prose, there is still the expectation that the dissertation will sound scholarly. Your dissertation should *not* sound like an informal essay or an editorial; it has to sound like the writing of a scholar. Furthermore, scholars write in a style that is formal, not colloquial, and is objective, not subjective. The letter writer says, "We've had a lot of rain these past few weeks." The scholar writes, "Rainfall for the period June 1–30, 2009 was measured at 10.2 inches, 3.6 inches above the seasonal average (Shew, 2010)."

Dissertations are also organized in a special way. Although there is increasing variation in how dissertations are organized, most still follow this time-honored pattern: Introduction, Review of the Literature, Methodology, Results, and Summary and Discussion. Even those who vary from this standard pattern follow a predictable order in which the variations are minor: tell what problem you studied; explain how you studied it; report the results; summarize and discuss the findings.

Dissertations tend to follow very specific rules about matters of style. Although instructors vary in their requirements for handling tables, writing headings, and documenting sources, there is much less variation tolerated in dissertations. Every profession has its preferred style guide, and dissertations are expected to follow those guides religiously. One of the first things to check with your dissertation chair is the style guide preferred, since most universities have their own guidelines. (Throughout this book the term *chair* is used to designate the faculty member primarily responsible for directing the research and guiding the writing of the dissertation; in many universities the terms *adviser* or *director* may also be used for this role.)

MAKING ETHICAL CHOICES WITH RESPECT TO THE DISSERTATION

There are several ethical considerations to keep in mind as you do your research and report your results.

Conduct Ethical Research

First, you must be certain that the study is consistent with generally accepted ethical principles. The following principles should be kept in mind at all times:

- Equity. The study does not reflect or support discrimination based on age, ethnicity, gender, sexual orientation, social class, or disability.

- Honesty. The study is characterized by honesty and openness. If the study requires deception, the researcher should be sure that the results will warrant the deception, that there are no alternative methods available, and that those deceived are informed as soon as possible. (See the American Psychological Association's [APA] Certification of Compliance with APA Ethical Principles. A copy of the APA Ethical Principles concerning research may be obtained from http://www.apa.org/ethics/.)
- Humane consideration. The study does not require or result in emotional or physical pain for participants.

Secure Informed Consent

You also should be sure to secure the informed consent of participants. The term *participants* is broadly used here to mean any who are involved in your research. Suppose, for example, that you wish to conduct a study in a local high school of the effectiveness of a program designed to improve students' self-esteem. Here are all those who should give their informed consent: the school board, the school principal, the teachers whose classes will be involved, and any experts whom you ask to review the materials. You should also secure the approval of students and their parents, if students' instructional program(s) will be significantly affected. All those individuals should know what you will study, which methods you will use, and why you are conducting the study. Knowing that teachers are sometimes reluctant to complete surveys for dissertations, some graduate students will conceal that fact, pretending that the study is being done solely for professional reasons. To act in this matter is clearly unethical.

Securing informed consent is generally interpreted to mean that you will provide at the outset honest answers to the following questions:

- What will be studied?
- Why is it being studied? Indicate here that the study is being undertaken as a degree requirement.
- What methods will be used?
- Who will participate, and why have they been selected?
- What are the benefits from the study itself?
- What are the potential risks, if any?
- What is the time commitment required?
- Is any compensation anticipated?
- Is there an assurance of confidentiality? If you have told participants that their identity will be kept confidential, then you must maintain that confidentiality.

A standard form can be developed and then provided to all involved. One example is shown in Exhibit 1.1.

Acknowledge All Those Who Have Contributed or Collaborated

Another issue that needs to be dealt with at the outset is that of originality and collaboration. In your work as a graduate student, you will often work closely with and receive the help of other students and members of the faculty. Such professional collaboration has a long and honored tradition and has been the source of significant professional accomplishments. However, such relationships also raise a central issue of professional integrity. No written guidelines can ever cover all the delicate issues of who deserves credit for what. Perhaps the best guideline is one of simple honesty: *Never claim credit for work that is not yours, and always give full credit to those who have helped you.* The following advice is offered for dealing with some specific problems that frequently arise, both with the dissertation and with other academic papers.

Exhibit 1.1 Sample Information Form

Title of Study: Assessment Instruction: Secondary English Teachers' Problems and Successes

Problem to Be Studied: What difficulties do secondary English teachers experience and what successes do they achieve as they try to design instruction based on performance assessments?

Rationale for Study: Secondary English educators throughout the nation are attempting to forge a closer relationship between performance assessment and teaching. Two initial studies indicate that student achievement improves when the linkages are strengthened. However, only one study to date has documented what happens when teachers try to use assessment-driven instruction. The study will be completed as the basis for a master's thesis in English education.

Methodology: Two secondary English teachers will be selected for the study. They will be asked to keep a log of their experiences. Their students will complete two surveys (attached as Figures 1 and 2). The researcher will interview the teachers on three occasions—once in September, once in January, and once in May.

Participants: Two secondary English teachers who have been trained in assessment-driven instruction will be selected from volunteers. Neither their names nor the names of the district or the school will be identified in the study. One of their classes will also participate in the study.

Benefits and Risks: The benefits are both professional and personal. The study should add to the knowledge base for an important development in teaching. The teachers who participate will receive feedback about their attempts to use this new method. There are no risks involved to the teachers or their students—no more than minimal risk.

Time Commitment and Compensation: The total time commitment from the secondary English teachers is expected to be ten hours of their preparation or out-of-school time. Student surveys will require a half hour of class time. No one will be compensated for participating.

1. Remember that the dissertation is expected to be an individual effort. Joint authorship is usually discouraged. If your university permits collaborative research for graduate degrees, then you should state explicitly the nature of the collaboration and secure the written approval of your committee.

2. Document all facts and ideas that are not commonly known and that are not original with you. This is the basic rule, of course. The following simple admonition might be added: When in doubt, document. Keep in mind that some plagiarism is often unintentional: You have read some theoretical work, its ideas seem interesting, you remember the ideas but forget the source, and when you are writing the idea reappears in the facade of an original conception. The obvious way to avoid unintentional plagiarism is to note the source when the idea first comes into your awareness. Also, be sure to document all paraphrases and direct quotations, of course. These matters are more fully discussed throughout the book.

3. Accept the help of anyone who wants to edit your work, but acknowledge the assistance in the front matter of the paper or dissertation. All writers (including these authors) need an editor; no one is a good judge of his or her own writing. But remember that editing involves minor correcting; it is not rewriting. Don't let another student—or a professor—rewrite your materials for you, unless that person wants to appear as a coauthor. There obviously is a very fine line between editing and rewriting; your conscience is the best judge of where that line falls.

4. Secure written permission to use or quote any entire works that have been published elsewhere. Most publishers do not expect you to secure permission

to quote excerpts for critical or scholarly purposes; however, you should secure permission if you reproduce a work such as a poem, short story, entire table, or figure, or if you plan to use someone else's questionnaire or survey instrument.

5. Acknowledge all assistance received. In the "acknowledgments" section of your dissertation, you should acknowledge the assistance of anyone who has helped you with the content or the writing. You should acknowledge as well any outside financial assistance you have received in support of the research. It usually is wise to show the wording of the proposed acknowledgment to the person whose help is being acknowledged. Such checking prevents the embarrassment of giving too much credit to a professor (for example) who would rather not be credited or who might feel your acknowledgment should be expressed less effusively.

6. Observe scholarly norms in listing joint authorship in any articles you publish. When more than one individual has contributed substantially to the work, that work should be published under joint authorship. In articles published under joint authorship, the authors are usually listed in the order of their contribution: the author chiefly responsible for the article is listed first; the author second in importance, second; and so on.

Report the Results Honestly and Objectively

Obviously the most important ethical issue is not to fudge your results. Remember that in the most basic sense there are no failed studies if they are completed carefully; even negative results are important and add to existing knowledge. Also guard against the temptation to shade the language or let your biases be apparent.

Securing the Needed Resources

The other preliminary matter that you must consider is being sure that you have the resources you need.

Analyze Your Needs

First, determine whether you will have the time needed to complete a winning dissertation. Ideally, you should have sufficient funds so that you can work on the dissertation full-time. If that is not possible, then you will have to find a way to become a "time manager" by setting aside extended blocks of time for your research and writing. You cannot write a winning dissertation in one-hour stints; you need extended time periods that will enable you to prepare, research, write, and revise.

The second key resource is hardware. You should have easy access to a powerful computer, adequate data storage, and a laser printer. Although it is possible to hire someone to do your word processing for you, it is not a good answer when considering your long-term professional career needs. Professors and educational leaders must learn to do their own word processing. With the continuing advancement of technology, the preparation of the dissertation is much easier than 10 to 20 years ago.

The third important resource is money. The budget worksheet shown in Exhibit 1.2 may help you make some estimates of the funds you will need. The items are explained briefly below.

Tuition and Fees

You have to pay tuition for any courses you still must take. In addition, most graduate schools require you to pay a fee during the terms when you are working on your dissertation. Although some students complain about such fees, dissertation advising is a labor-intensive process, and your fees cover only a part of the costs.

Exhibit 1.2 Budget Worksheet

Item	Your Estimate
1. Tuition and Fees	_____
2. Consulting Services	_____
3. Hardware, Software, Other Equipment	_____
4. Paper and Other Supplies	_____
5. Books, Journals, Monographs	_____
6. Telephone, Fax, Postage	_____
7. Copying	_____
8. Travel	_____
Total Needed	_____

Consulting Fees

You should determine whether you will have to pay for any of these services: stipend for participants, word processing, data entry, data analysis, editing, and copying.

Hardware, Software, and Other Equipment

As explained previously, you will need access to a powerful computer with adequate data storage and auxiliary data storage devices, and a laser printer. You may also need software for word processing and data analysis. Special projects may require other equipment such as a camcorder, camera, scanner, VCR, and DVD player or recorder.

Paper and Other Supplies

You will find that you consume printer paper at a high rate as you write and revise.

Books, Journals, and Monographs

Even if you have access to an excellent library, you will probably want to purchase some basic references so that you can make notes in the margins and keep them always accessible.

Telephone, Fax, and Postage

These are essential communication costs that mount as you do your research and send chapters to your committee. However, the cost of such communication is being greatly reduced with the use of e-mail, Skype, and other Internet-based communication.

Copying

You may need to make copies of instruments; you will certainly make multiple copies of each chapter. However, costs associated with photocopying may be reduced if your committee accepts an electronic version of the document.

Travel

If your research requires you to make on-site visits to distant locations, you will need a substantial travel budget. Yet with continued technological advancements and the use of the Internet, travel may not be perceived as necessary.

Also keep in mind that other students may provide a helpful resource. Some students have found it helpful to develop a support group composed of students who have reached the dissertation stage. Students reported that such a group was helpful to them in dealing with dissertation problems (D'Belcher, 2005; Melroy, 1994, 2002).

Search for Special Support

If you find that your needs exceed your resources, you should search systematically for special support. The first place to turn is to apply for a graduate assistantship. A graduate assistantship does more than provide you with extra funds: it enables you to work closely with faculty and staff, provides access to a scholarly network, and helps you develop the skills you need.

If a graduate assistantship is not available, consider applying for a grant from one of the foundations that support graduate research. The best source here is *The Foundation Directory Online* maintained by the Foundation Center (http://fconline.foundationcenter.org/).

UNDERSTANDING THE KEY DIFFERENCES BETWEEN THE THESIS AND THE DISSERTATION

As noted at the outset, the master's thesis and the doctoral dissertation are both reports of scholarly investigations, completed as part of the degree requirements. All the aforementioned attributes apply to both scholarly works. Although institutional requirements vary, there are some general differences that should be noted here.

First, most master's theses are more limited in scope and depth than doctoral dissertations. A master's thesis might report on a study of grouping as used in classrooms in a particular region; a doctoral dissertation might compare the effects of two grouping systems in teaching elementary mathematics. As a consequence of this difference, doctoral dissertations tend to be longer than master's theses.

Also, the doctoral dissertation is likely to be more rigorous in its research methodology than a master's thesis. The thesis is more likely to seem like a "project report," explaining, for example, how instruction was planned and organized prior to lesson delivery in a middle school. A doctoral dissertation on the same topic might be a detailed analysis of how teachers planned and organized instruction and how they used class time.

Noting these differences is not to depreciate the master's thesis as a scholarly work. Many make important contributions to the field.

ROLES AND RESPONSIBILITIES OF THE COMMITTEE

You first need to understand the roles and related responsibilities of the committee. Members of your dissertation committee are responsible for giving you the direction and assistance you need to complete the dissertation, but that responsibility does not mean that they are supposed to do any of the work for you. It does mean, however, that they should be available to you, within the limits of their other responsibilities. As members of the faculty, they are also responsible to the university to uphold the academic standards of that institution. This means that they cannot accept careless work just to enable you to finish your degree. As researchers and educators, they also feel a responsibility to the larger profession, to ensure that the dissertation makes a significant contribution to professional knowledge. As professors, they feel responsible to themselves and their career advancement. They have their own standards of quality and their own need to advance their careers. Finally, they have several personal roles that cause their own pressures—spouse, parent, and son or daughter.

Obviously, these are conflicting responsibilities that cause conscientious committee members to experience their own stress. For example, they want to be available to you, but they also need to research and publish if they are to receive tenure and be promoted. Or they want to help you finish in a reasonable time, but they believe that your dissertation needs much more work. They are reluctant to give you criticism that will result in your feeling negative about yourself or them, but at the same time they know that your work needs improvement. If you understand these conflicting responsibilities, you will be better able to deal with committee problems that develop.

THE DYNAMICS OF THE COMMITTEE

Each committee will vary somewhat, depending upon the personalities of the members. However, three well-documented features of academic life will clearly have an impact on committee dynamics.

First, academic life is hierarchical. As a consequence, dissertation committees are hierarchical, reflecting the status distinctions of academic life. Full professors are at the top. Tenured associate professors come next, followed by nontenured associates. Assistant professors have a lower status—except for graduate students, who have the lowest status of all. Length of service at that university also affects status: faculty who have had longer periods of service tend to receive higher status than those who have less. These status distinctions suggest that there will be fewer intracommittee conflicts if the chair has higher status than other committee members. If your chair is an associate professor and a committee member is a full professor, the status distinctions might complicate their committee relationships. The harsh fact is that because you have the lowest status of all, you do not have the power to ignore committee recommendations and decisions.

Also, academic life is individualistic. As a consequence, most committees are fragmented and individualistic. Higher education does not tend to reward cooperation and collaboration. Many faculty members are promoted and receive tenure chiefly on the basis of their research and publication, with their advising having much less weight. These features mean that members have no strong incentives to meet together and work together. Although your committee members may meet with each other at faculty and departmental meetings, they will not be discussing your dissertation at such encounters. In fact, most dissertation committees come together only infrequently, at and prior to defenses. This feature means that you probably have to find ways of working with them as individuals, not as a group.

Finally, academic life is somewhat rigidly structured, with fixed roles and distinctions. This rigid structure usually holds true in committee work, too. The chair is clearly in charge, and the other members understand that their role is to assist, while acknowledging the authority of the chair. It is the chair's reputation that is on the line when your dissertation is reviewed by other faculty, by the graduate school office, and by external members of the profession.

PREVENTING PROBLEMS WITH THE COMMITTEE

The key to positive relationships with the committee is preventing problems before they occur. You can do this in several ways. First, choose a committee whose members are compatible with each other and with you. Problems of relationships can often be avoided if you are sensitive to the matter when forming a committee. Thus, you, the dissertating student, should do your homework to determine the capability of likely professors to serve as committee members. You should review the completed dissertations from your department in the university library. While reviewing those completed dissertations, note those committee members whose names appear frequently. A dissertating student can learn those who work well together, because their names appear frequently on the dissertations' signature pages.

Second, at a very early stage in your work with the committee, clarify the nature of the committee's relationships with each other and with you. Most committees are structured in this fashion: The chair does most of the work involved in directing the research and the dissertation and is the primary contact with the student; a second member of the committee provides needed technical expertise; other committee members play a much less active role. Be sure you understand where you are expected to get the help you need—and how much help the committee wants to give you. Learn to use your committee without taking advantage of the members.

Next, determine the specific ground rules by which the committee expects to operate. At the proposal defense or immediately thereafter, you should consult with the chair and the rest of the committee, if necessary, to clarify all important procedural matters. It is to your advantage to obtain contact information from all committee members, and the information should be stored by you, the dissertating student, to use when communicating with the committee member or members.

Selecting a compatible committee and clarifying relationships and procedural matters should avert most of the difficulties that students encounter with their committees. The other suggestions for maintaining productive relationships with your committee can be summarized briefly:

- Do not appear for a conference without an appointment. Most university professors are busy people, contrary to the view of those who think that professors do not have much to do all day. They don't like being surprised by seeing a doctoral student at the office door, chapter in hand.
- Do not telephone the professor at home, unless directed otherwise. Most professors prefer to keep academic life and home life separate.
- Be sensitive to your committee's work schedules and vacation periods. If you feel you have to give the members a chapter to read over the spring break, make suitable apologies.
- When you mail materials, do so in a businesslike manner. Put your name and address on all correspondence and manuscripts. Never send original materials through the mail. Check with the

committee to determine if the use of e-mail is acceptable for receiving and responding to chapters. If so, ask the committee member's preference of word processing software to avoid any issues with the recipient's ability to open the e-mail attachment.

- Keep your committee informed about progress. A good general rule is this: *Do not let a month go by without contact.* Even a brief note on a postcard or an e-mail message will be a useful reminder that you are still working.

DEALING WITH COMMITTEE PROBLEMS

Even if you have followed all these suggestions, there will still be some predictable problems resulting from the above roles and characteristics that might affect your progress.

Committee Members Do Not Give Feedback Promptly

For most committee members, providing assistance to doctoral students is a labor-intensive responsibility, one that is rather low on their list of priorities. This means that some committee members will be slow in giving you feedback—not because they are irresponsible but because of the conflicting responsibilities. The unwritten norm is two weeks for committee members to provide feedback. Obviously this will vary, depending upon such factors as the academic calendar, professors' attendance at conferences, and their own involvement in research and publication.

When you experience what you feel are inordinate delays, you should deal with the problem differently, depending upon the source. If other committee members are slow in responding, e-mail a tactful reminder (without sending a copy to your chair, or if you decide to copy your chair, be sure that it is a blind copy) or telephone your concern. If they still do not respond, then simply report the facts to your chair and let him or her handle the problem.

What do you do if your chair is slow in responding to your chapters? First, as previously noted, you should attempt to clarify at the outset how much time is usually required; two weeks seems to be an unstated norm. The first few times you experience an inordinate delay, handle the matter as if you're a very tactful bill collector. Call and say, "I'm calling just to be sure you received Chapter 2; I haven't heard and was getting just a bit anxious. When do you think I might be receiving your comments on Chapter 2?" Then if you still haven't heard by the date indicated, call again: "I'm calling just to inquire if there's a special problem with Chapter 2; you indicated that I might be receiving it by today."

If those tactful phone calls do not have the desired effect, talk the problem over in a face-to-face discussion. Express an attitude that's reflected in these words:

> I know you're very busy, and I don't want to make unreasonable demands. However, I am feeling frustrated by my lack of progress. I thought it might be helpful if we could talk the matter over. I want to determine in what way I may be responsible for the delays and take appropriate action.

The rest of the discussion should maintain this problem-solving orientation: How can we cooperate to reduce the turnaround time?

Committee Members Give Conflicting Advice

Sometimes the conflicting advice is from two different committee members; sometimes it comes from a single professor who changes his or her mind.

If you receive conflicting advice from two members of your committee (including the chair), let the chair handle the matter. Explain the conflict to the chair and ask how you should resolve it. It is the chair's responsibility to mediate such differences; you should not be in the middle.

The problem of receiving conflicting advice from one individual is common. Dissertation students often justifiably complain that after they have revised a chapter according to their chair's (or committee member's) recommendations, they receive more revision suggestions from the same individual that conflict with those first received.

Here is a good process to use that will avoid this frustrating experience.

1. Always check to be sure that you understand the feedback received and have a written record of it. If you meet in a conference, summarize the conference in a written memo and send a copy to the professor: "Included in this e-mail is a summary of my notes of the changes we discussed on Nov. 2, 2011. I want to be sure my record is accurate." If you get a written response, call to clarify any ambiguities. You have to be sure that you understand correctly what the professor wants you to do.

2. When you have revised according to the professor's suggestions, send the professor a copy of his or her suggestions with the revised chapter when it is forwarded. That helps the professor remember what was said and reduces the amount of conflicting advice.

Committee Members Give Unhelpful Advice

You may receive what you consider to be unhelpful advice or editorial comments. If the advice or comments are too general, call and ask for specifics. If you feel that you received counterproductive advice about a relatively common matter, accept it. It is not worth arguing over. However, if you feel that the matter is important, deal with the difference in a professional manner. If the unproductive advice comes from a committee member other than the chair, ask the chair to help you resolve the matter. If the unproductive advice comes from the chair, then meet to review the matter. In essence, communicate with the chair on a regular basis.

Relationships Critically Deteriorate

In a few unfortunate instances, graduate students find that their relationship with the chair or some other committee member deteriorates so badly that they feel the conflict is interfering with their progress. If the conflict is with some member other than the chair, ask for a meeting with just you and the member. In that conference, emphasize that you wish to solve a problem, not complain or blame. Use a problem-solving mode that makes these points:

- I have the impression that there are some serious problems between us. What is your perception?
- I believe these are the specific difficulties. What is your perception?
- These difficulties are causing me some serious problems in my progress.
- How do you think we might solve the problems together?

If that face-to-face conference does not solve the problem, you should ask the chair to intervene.

If the problem is with the chair, you should use the same problem-solving approach in trying to resolve the difficulties in a private conference. It is probably unwise to ask another committee member to intercede on your behalf in this instance; doing so may place the member in an untenable position with the chair.

If you are convinced that the chair or a member should be replaced, be sure to handle the matter professionally. In doing so, keep in mind three useful guidelines:

- Use a face-to-face discussion rather than writing. Writing about a problem usually makes it worse, since it is a one-way communication.
- Observe the university's chain of command. Work with a committee member before going to the chair. Work with the chair before going to the department chair. Try to resolve the matter with the department chair before going to the dean of your school. In extreme cases, work with your school's dean before complaining to the dean of the graduate school.
- Accept the fact that conflict is endemic to the faculty-student relationship. You each have different perspectives, values, and goals. Differences are bound to arise. Accept all the minor ones as part of your struggle to achieve the degree. Resolve all differences in a professional manner, even when you feel that others are taking advantage of you.

Solving Personal Problems With the Dissertation

You will also experience some personal problems in completing the dissertation. There is a small body of research and a large body of anecdotal evidence indicating that doctoral students experience some common problems throughout the dissertation processes. (For the research, see the following: Council of Graduate Schools, 1991; Germeroth, 1990; Huguley, 1989; Tadeusik, 1989; Whitted, 1987; the Writing Center at the University of North Carolina at Chapel Hill, 2012.) Since the common problems seem to occur at specified times in the dissertation process, they are discussed here according to the stages during which they usually develop.

These problems can be crippling in their effects. Some estimates indicate that only 40 percent of all doctoral students ever finish. Although "dropping out" is often a result of financial and work-related factors, the emotional stresses associated with completing the dissertation undoubtedly play an important role. For a few students, these stresses will be serious enough to warrant professional counseling; for such individuals, no book can suffice. For the rest, however, some rational analysis of the problems and their solutions might be useful.

There seem to be four crucial periods when doctoral students experience serious emotional problems that relate to the dissertation: near the end of the course work, after completing course work and before writing the proposal, after the proposal hearing, and after the dissertation defense.

Problems Near the End of Course Work

A large proportion of doctoral students withdraw from the program near the end of their course work. In many instances the reasons are valid ones, and withdrawal from the program is the wiser choice. They change career plans, choosing to follow a career where the doctorate is not essential. Their values and their priorities change; they decide that family, job, or personal enjoyment is more important than the prestige of having the doctorate.

Many simply do not have the money: Graduate education is becoming so expensive that many of the most promising students are withdrawing because they have grown tired of mortgaging their futures. Others withdraw primarily for emotional reasons; it is fear that most of all gives rise to the problems at this stage. From lack of knowledge and from their own insecurity, many doctoral students have come to fear the dissertation. They may try to conceal this fear by pretending that the degree is unimportant and the dissertation absurd—but it is there all the same, despite the forms it takes. The specific fears seem to be several.

"I'm afraid that the dissertation will just take too much time." This is a general fear that seems to color all other feelings. The dissertation seems like an impassable mountain; you probably have heard stories of students who have struggled for years without ever finishing. To a certain extent, this fear is justified; from choosing a topic to defending the dissertation can take as long as two or three years for part-time students. However, even a complex project like writing a dissertation can be accomplished efficiently with careful planning and conscientious effort; it is like a long journey that you make one step at a time.

The scheduling suggestions offered in Chapter 6 should help you cope with this particular anxiety. In addition, the following suggestions should help:

- Follow the schedule, even if it means making other adjustments.
- If you encounter obstacles, get the help you need.
- Break larger tasks into smaller steps.
- Keep in close touch with your academic adviser and dissertation chair.

"I'm afraid I don't have what it takes to do the dissertation." That is also a reasonable fear, since writing the dissertation is a demanding task. The way to deal with this fear is to assess your capabilities as objectively as you can, with the help of a faculty member whom you respect and who knows you. Do not ask a spouse or a friend, "Do I have what it takes?" You will probably receive only well-intentioned encouragement.

Instead, do a systematic assessment of your strengths and weaknesses with input from someone who can be honest with you; the form in Exhibit 1.3 (see page 30) might be of help to you here. If you identify deficiencies, take steps to remedy them, if they seem remediable.

"I'm afraid of what the dissertation will do to my family and social life." There is also a modicum of rationality in this

anxiety. Dissertations take time, money, and mental energy, and many relationships have been strained during dissertation time. Here again there is an obvious solution. Instead of simply worrying about the matter, discuss it openly with your spouse. Examine together what mutual advantages will accrue from receiving the degree and what sacrifices must be made. How much will the dissertation cost in money—and where will the money come from? How will doing the dissertation affect the contributions you can make to child rearing and household maintenance? Can your spouse understand and accept the fact that you will often seem distracted, absorbed, moody, and perhaps irritable, especially on those bad days when you get back a chapter your chair has rejected?

"I'm worried about the financial costs of doing the dissertation." The budgeting process suggested earlier should be of help here. Be realistic about the costs of doing the dissertation and about the resources available to you.

"I'm worried about the impact on my professional assignment." At the outset of the entire process, discuss your plans with your supervisor, without asking for special treatment. If it seems feasible, choose a research topic that will be of help to your organization. As you experience conflicts between writing the dissertation and doing your job, try to find win-win solutions by making compromises and adjustments.

There are some real fears to be confronted and dealt with, but they are all surmountable.

Problems at the End of Course Work

Another critical period is after you have completed the course work and before you get to the proposal stage. Students who withdraw at this point are the army of the ABD's—all but the dissertation. Again, there are often practical reasons operating: lack of money, change of plans, the

Exhibit 1.3 Crucial Dissertation Skills and Traits

Doctoral student's name: _____

Assessor: _____

Directions: The student named above would like your candid assessment of his or her specific abilities, as they relate to completing the dissertation. For each crucial skill or trait listed below, circle one of the following:

NP: No problem here with this skill.

IM: Some improvement is needed here, but the skill or trait can be remedied.

SD: Seriously deficient; the deficiency seems so serious that it may be a major stumbling block.

THE SKILL OR TRAIT AND YOUR RATING			
1. Work habits: can set and stick to a work schedule; can work for long periods of time without close monitoring or direction; can work efficiently without wasting time.	NP	IM	SD
2. Writing: can write good academic prose; knows conventions of academic writing; can write clearly.	NP	IM	SD
3. Organizing and planning: can set long-term and short-term goals; can develop systematic plans to meet those goals; can take corrective action when problems are encountered.	NP	IM	SD
4. Research: understands the limitations and uses of the research method selected; can use that research methodology in scholarly fashion without close monitoring.	NP	IM	SD
5. Intellectual: reasons logically; understands complexities of research issues; can critique and synthesize the research of others; can learn from experience.	NP	IM	SD
6. Interpersonal: takes criticism well; accepts direction when necessary; is sensitive to faculty priorities.	NP	IM	SD

onset of health problems. More often, however, the problems are emotional and psychological ones. The problems at this stage all seem related to a pervasive anxiety that results in prolonged procrastination. Notice how this student put it in a candid letter to a friend who asked about his progress:

> I've been paying my dissertation fees for five terms now and I still don't have a proposal ready. I keep promising myself that this will be the term when I get the proposal in shape—but I never make it. I just can't seem to get a fix on a good problem—everything important either has been studied already or is too big for me to handle. I make lists of problems—but nothing clicks. I talk to the professors and each one suggests a different problem until I'm completely confused. And I don't think I have the research skills I need; I have always been weak in statistics. I guess, to be honest, if I did find a problem and could feel positive about my skills, I would still have trouble developing a proposal—I just don't know where to begin. Some students talk about 150-page proposals. How could I ever write 150 pages about what I will study?

A statement like this reflects anxieties that most ABD's have at one time or another. Aside from being colored by the general fears described previously, the statement reveals some specific concerns about the topic, the research skills, and the proposal. How to deal with these specific concerns is to a great extent the focus of this entire work. However, some general guidance can be offered at this point for dealing with dissertation anxiety and the resultant sense of being immobilized.

1. Decide once and for all whether you want the doctor's degree. If you don't, withdraw gracefully, consoling yourself with the fact that most great leaders and artists never had the doctorate. If you do want the degree, then make the necessary plans and do it.

2. Find one professor who is willing to work with you as a chair. At a certain point, some students can be helped by talking with several professors, questioning them about research problems and methodologies. But if you are stuck at the preproposal stage, you are probably better off asking one professor who you hope will be your chair. Be candid about your problem: "I'm having trouble getting to the proposal stage. I'd like to work with you, but I'll need your help in getting myself organized." Listen to that one professor; talking to several professors about possible topics and methods will only confuse and delay you.

3. With the assistance of your chair and this book, choose a topic that you want to study and settle on the methodology. Stop thinking about the 10 topics that you might study; settle on one. *Don't become obsessed with finding the perfect topic; like the perfect spouse, it doesn't exist.*

4. Read a few completed dissertations on a topic of interest. It helps to see some completed works to gain a realistic perspective about the dissertation. You may also get some ideas that will stimulate your thinking.

5. Develop any skills that need sharpening. If you feel a bit weak with the research method, get the necessary tutoring or instruction. If you are unsure about your writing skills, ascertain what services the university provides to students needing assistance.

6. Develop a schedule and stick to it. By conferring with your chair and applying what you learn in this book, develop a realistic schedule and force yourself to meet the deadlines you have set.

Your choices are clear: You can withdraw gracefully; you can continue to enrich the university's coffers by paying your fees without making progress; or you can get your act together. It is as simple as that. Just stop making excuses to yourself.

Problems After the Proposal

All students writing dissertations experience several emotional highs and lows. Your data gathering goes well, and you feel euphoric. You get a chapter back with some caustic criticisms, and you feel crushed. A good part of being able to deal with the emotional problems encountered during the dissertation itself is knowing what form they will take and being prepared to deal with them. For the most part, the problems at the dissertation stage seem to be ones of doubt and uncertainty that take the form of predictable complaints.

"I'm tired." Common complaints are physical and psychic fatigue; you just get very tired collecting data, sitting at the desk, pounding the keys. Your head starts to hurt, and you find yourself feeling irritable. You know the answers to fatigue: eat sensibly, exercise, get adequate rest, and reward yourself with a day off now and then.

"The data gathering is not going well." All researchers, from the beginner to the expert, encounter predictable problems with the research itself. Questionnaires are not returned, subjects leave the study, instruments do not work as they should, or the data don't act the way you predicted. The answer to such problems, obviously, is immediate communication with your chair. Do not wait, hoping things will be corrected; even if they are, your chair will want to know about and assist with the difficulties as they develop. And do not avoid confrontation, fearing that your chair will tell you to scrap the whole thing. Good chairs know how to salvage studies that start to go wrong. Moreover, in a scientific sense there are no failures in well-designed studies; "no significant difference" may be truly a significant finding.

"I keep finding references in the literature I want to cite." It is a wise idea to keep abreast of current research as you do your study, but once you have reviewed the research for your dissertation, there usually is no need to add very current references. You can add current references to your own files and review them prior to the hearing, but it would be unwise to continue revising the literature chapter once it has been approved—unless you come across some truly important study that just cannot be ignored. Confer with your chair to set a reasonable date for concluding the search of the literature—in other words, when to cease with the literature review.

"I will be the last of my cohort to finish." Such comparisons are inevitable but irrelevant: Writing a dissertation is not like running a race. All that matters is the quality of the work. Four or five years from now no one will remember who finished first and who last.

"I now feel that I chose the wrong topic." This doubt seems to beset all doctoral students at some point. Just remember that there is no right topic and get on with concluding your study of the one you chose.

"I have writer's block and can't write." Dry periods come to all who write. The best answer for writer's block is to write: Sit at the word processor and force yourself to write, even though the product is not of the highest quality. You can always go back and revise. What you should not do about writer's block is worry about it while you find excuses for not writing.

"I'm worried sick about the defense." Reassure yourself with the knowledge that very few students fail the defense; a good chair won't let you go to the defense until he or she is sure you are ready. Also, if you follow the suggestions in this book, you should have no problems at the defense. It will seem more like a final ritual of celebration than a test.

Note that most of those complaints seem to have a common thread of self-doubt, and that self-doubt is understandable. You feel tired. The end is not yet in sight. You are not getting much positive feedback. You seem close to the end of your resources. You are like a runner who feels tired at the halfway mark. At such a time you need to turn to whatever support is available—your peers, your chair, your spouse, your spiritual director—to help you find the inner resources to continue. Most doctoral students find support in networking with others at the same stage.

Problems After the Defense

Most students find it difficult to believe that there can be any emotional problems after the defense, but many who have gone through the experience talk about the period right after the defense as a time of "postpartum depression." It seems to be a general sense of emptiness, of bleak uncertainty.

The causes are understandable. There is first a predictable letdown. The doctor's degree really has not changed things, and having "doctor" in front of your name has not markedly increased the respect that people accord you. You probably face some career dislocation. You pursued the doctorate because you wanted to advance professionally. Now you have the degree, and you face the trauma of job hunting. And there is often a sense of emptiness in each week. A major intellectual task that gave your days an organizing center is finished, and you have all that time now to use in some productive fashion. Maybe now you are no longer the center of attention in the household; that patient spouse who sacrificed for so long now expects you to carry more than half the load. And you take a look at your dissertation in its new binder and shake your head in dismay: it really wasn't worth it after all.

The best way out of such depression is usually through meaningful action. After a suitable period of self-indulgence, decide what you want to do next professionally. Will you continue with your research? Will you publish from your dissertation? Will you try to develop a part-time consulting role? Will you actively seek a new position? Then make the plans that will help you accomplish what now seems important to you.

A Look Ahead

The rest of this book will take you through the complex process of writing the dissertation. Although the suggestions have been drawn from considerable experience in helping students produce winning dissertations, be sure that you check closely with your dissertation chair every step along the way.

Technology Technique: The Role of the Internet for Research in the Dissertation Process

The availability of the Internet has made and continues to make the "dissertating" process easier. Today's graduate students now have the ability to search for relevant information from any device that is able to connect to the Internet—smart phones, tablets, laptop computers, and desktop computers. Searching for information is easier and quicker; however, one major concern is the credibility of the information located.

In today's technological world, it is quite a simple task to upload information to the Internet. Anyone can create and upload a document to an Internet location without scrutiny; therefore, the quality and believability of such information needs to be considered by the reader of such information. The credibility of the information is enhanced if a reference list or bibliography is published with the document. As with all sources of information, graduate students need to be certain that the facts purported in such Internet documents are reliable before accepting the information for use in the dissertation (Wehmeyer, 1995). For determining the credibility of Internet information, if similar information is found in three sources, it is presumed to be credible.

Doctoral committee members who are concerned with maintaining academic standards question the use of the Internet. One reason is the credibility of the information. Another reason is the belief by some faculty that credible research can only be found in the library; and those faculty members think that dissertating students must spend multiple hours reviewing the actual journals, manuscripts, theses, dissertations, and so on in their hard copy formats in a campus facility. Thus, dissertating students should discuss the use of the Internet as a research tool first with their chairs. After determining their chair's point of view, a conversation may be needed with the doctoral committee.

Dealing With Institutional Requirements

O ften, dealing with institutional requirements may be frustrating. This frustration may be the result of a lack of understanding or simply taking the time to become familiar with the institution's requirements for the research document. In general, you become so involved in your research that you may forget about the guidelines set forth by the institution regarding the degree completion requirements. The knowledge of institutional requirements will help facilitate a positive experience and successful completion of the research study.

STYLES

The style of the study may be institution specific, department specific, or dissertation chair specific. Regardless of the style, the information included in the study and the rigor of the study remain unchanged.

In terms of a specific style, for example, the dissertation may be completed using a traditional five-chapter model or a nontraditional four-chapter model. Both styles contain the same information with a slight variation of content within the chapters. For example, in the four-chapter dissertation style, Chapter One would include similar information as Chapters One and Two in a five-chapter dissertation style (see Exhibit 2.1).

SPECIFIC UNIVERSITY GUIDELINES OR REQUIREMENTS

Institutions of higher education have specific guidelines outlining how theses and dissertations are to be formatted and submitted as well as deadlines regulating what needs to transpire at certain intervals during the process.

All the specific information may be typically found within a graduate school's handbook, and it should also be available from the specific department in which you are studying for the degree.

Formatting. The institution usually follows a preferred style as dictated by guidelines set forth by organizations such as the American Psychological Association (APA), the Modern Language Association (MLA), and the Chicago Manuel of Style (CMS). Each of these styles of writing offers a unique way of formatting text, margins, fonts, and text style. Each of the aforementioned organizations may have specific information accessed via the Internet as well as by your local bookstore and/or university student bookstore.

Submission. The submission of your study is also specific to your institution's guidelines. There are two formal submissions: the proposal defense and the final defense. The proposal defense serves as a formal presentation of your work outlining how you propose to conduct the study. Typically, most institutions and/or specific departments require a minimum of two-week notification to the university community.

Exhibit 2.1 Comparison of Dissertation Formats

Traditional Five-Chapter Dissertation Format	Four-Chapter Dissertation Format

Chapter One—Introduction
 	
• Need for the Study
• Statement of the Problem
• Purpose of the Study
• Significance of the Study
• Research Questions and Hypotheses
• Overview of Methodology
• Definition of Terms
• Limitations/ Delimitations of the Study
• Assumptions
• Research Organization
 	
Chapter Two—Review of Related Literature
 	
• Themes
• Subthemes
• Summary
	Chapter One—Historical Perspective
	
	• Historical Overview
	• Statement of the Problem
	• Purpose of the Study
	• Significance of the Study
	• Review of Related Literature
	  o Themes
	  o Subthemes
	  o Summary
	• Methodological Assumptions
	• Methodological Limitations
	• Research Perspectives (Questions)?

Chapter Three—Research Design/Methodology
 	
• The Population
  o The Setting
  o The Background
  o Participants
• Design of the Study
  o Research Design
  o Instrumentation
    ▪ Pilot Study and Analysis
    ▪ Validity
	Chapter Two—Research Methodology
	
	• Research Design
	• Research Method
	  o Overview
	• Data Collection Procedures
	  o Participants
	    ▪ Techniques
	    ▪ Limitations
	    ▪ Analysis

Traditional Five-Chapter Dissertation Format	Four Chapter Dissertation Format
<ul><li>Reliability</li><li>Description</li></ul><ul><li>Threats to Internal and External Validity</li></ul><ul><li>Data Collection Procedures<ul><li>Processes</li><li>Directions</li><li>Controls</li></ul></li><li>Analysis of Data<ul><li>Demographics</li><li>Statistical Analyses</li><li>Data Collection Techniques/Tools</li></ul></li><li>Summary</li></ul>	
Chapter Four—Data Analysis<ul><li>Participants' Characteristics (Demographics)</li><li>Research Questions/ Null Hypotheses<ul><li>Analysis (for each)<ul><li>Findings (for each)</li></ul></li></ul></li><li>Summary</li></ul>	**Chapter Three—Data Analysis**<ul><li>Summary of Methodology<ul><li>Participants</li></ul></li><li>Demographics</li><li>Findings</li></ul>
Chapter Five—Discussion and Conclusions<ul><li>Summary</li><li>Procedures<ul><li>Findings</li><li>Demographics</li></ul></li><li>Research Questions/ Null Hypotheses</li><li>Conclusions</li><li>Implications</li><li>Recommendations</li></ul>	**Chapter Four—Discussion and Conclusions**<ul><li>Historical Perspective (Summary)</li><li>Statement of the Problem</li><li>Limitations/ Delimitations of the Study</li><li>Research Design and Methodology (Summary)<ul><li>Design</li></ul></li></ul>

(Continued)

(Continued)

Traditional Five-Chapter Dissertation Format	Four-Chapter Dissertation Format

	o Setting
	o Processes/ Procedures
	o Controls for Threats
	o Internal Validity
	o External Validity
	• Data Collection and Analysis
	• Findings (Summary)
	  o Demographics
	  o Research Questions/ Null Hypotheses
	  o Statistical Analysis
	  o Results
	• Conclusions
	• Implications
	• Recommendations

References	References
Appendices	Appendices

The final defense has several additional submission requirements; the document is approved by various officials within the department and the university. For example, once the study has been formally approved by your dissertation committee, all revisions are completed, and it has been signed by your dissertation chair, the study is submitted to the chair of the department in which your degree resides for his or her approval. The chair of the department then approves the document and forwards it to the graduate school for approval of the graduate school dean. The graduate school dean approves and notifies the student that all approval signatures have been obtained and the document is thereby accepted by the institution and ready for submission to the institution's organizations for completed studies (i.e., university library, ProQuest, respective department). Again, knowing beforehand expectations of the institution's submission process is important so that you will be able to facilitate a smooth study closure.

INSTITUTIONAL REVIEW BOARD

Universities that require Institutional Review Board (IRB) training and approval are commonly associated with institutions that have health-related schools and/or colleges as well as the social sciences including psychology, sociology, and anthropology. The purpose of the IRB training and approval process is to inform researchers of best practices in research methods related to the protection and welfare of the study participants as well as the investigator(s).

All research studies conducted at institutions require IRB approval of the study. This approval must be obtained by the Investigator(s) before they may collect any data. Each institution has a formal IRB approval process that is required at the beginning of the study and at the conclusion of the study.

With most research studies, the student, in consultation with and with the approval of his or her study chair, will submit the IRB approval form to the chair of the department in which the degree resides for the department chair's approval. Once the study has been approved at the department level, the study is forwarded to the IRB office for review and approval. Typically, the approval process takes approximately two weeks depending on the structure of the institution's IRB meetings and reviews process. This approval time line has been shortened quite a bit by institutions that have implemented an electronic approval process. Therefore, all forms (signatures/approval) are transmitted electronically resulting in a decrease of "lag" time created by campus mail systems.

Once the research study has been completed, the principal investigator has up to six months to submit an IRB "closure" form to the respective institution's IRB office. This IRB closure form is notification to the IRB office that the study has been completed and there no longer exists a need to continue examining the research question(s).

On a related note, if the study needs to remain open for an extended amount of time or if the nature of the submitted study protocol needs to be changed, then an IRB submission noting a review of the proposal must be submitted for continued approval so that you may continue to collect and analyze data.

Knowledge Requirements (Training)

The knowledge and training acquired by participating in the IRB training modules is important to understanding the ethical treatment of participants as well as the access and storage of data collected. As a student, I think the most valuable "oh hey" moment is the realization and understanding that the IRB process is meant to protect the researcher and participants. With this mind-set, the entire IRB process fits into a more logical and meaningful experience.

The IRB registration and tracking for training has greatly improved over the past years. Presently, students may access the website provided by their respective institution to register their IRB account. Typically, this registration is at no cost to the student. Once you have registered, you will be assigned an IRB number. You may use this number to stay updated on your certification and history of IRB training.

The initial IRB certification training consists of five online content modules. Each module is content specific, and the complete training covers topics ranging from the treatment of subjects to the collection and storing of data. At the end of each module, a test is provided that relates to the specific content covered within that module. Students are required to answer a set of multiple choice questions. You must score a minimum of 80 percent correct on each module to receive credit for the module and thus receive the certification to conduct a research study.

Upon successful completion of the training modules, you will receive a certificate of which you may print a hard copy. You may also access your file by using your IRB number to view when you last completed the certification modules.

Once you receive this IRB certification, it does not mean that you are never required to participate in ongoing training. In fact, the certification expires after a specific time interval, which we will discuss in the next section.At a point in time when you need to update your certification, you simply access the IRB website and input your IRB number; this will access your IRB personal site so that you may review your specific information. Because you need the "refresher" IRB training, you follow the links that will access those training modules. The IRB refresher module training is not as in-depth or as lengthy as the initial IRB training certification. This recertification allows for updates and best practices in research and serves as a valuable update of information.

Certificate Time Frame

The IRB certificate time frame is three years. Therefore, if you continue to engage in active research or it takes you longer than three years to complete your study, you must update your certification (per the discussion in the previous section). Unfortunately, the IRB site will not notify you of the expiration of your certification; you must find a way to remember this frame so that you are not caught in an awkward situation of engaging in research without being certified to do so.

DEGREE COMPLETION TIME LINES

Before beginning your graduate program of study at an institution, it is wise to ascertain the institution's program completion time limit. This information is important as you map your program of study requirements concerning coursework and research to your personal and professional obligations. The degree time limit may help you focus and plot your strategy within the allotted amount of time so that you may know your commitment required and gain valuable experience associated with the program.

Institutions vary on the length of time of degree completion. Generally, most institutions' degree completion timelines range from a minimum of six years to a maximum of ten years. Also, with most institutions, there is some flexibility within the time line requirements to allow for time extensions if needed. For example, an institution with a six-year degree completion time line may allow for two one-year extensions without you having to do anything other than submit a request for the extension along with a valid reason. For the most part, time extensions likely to be considered, and approved, by the institution are for issues such as illness, change of job, or other personal or professional life challenges that may have prevented someone from completing the degree within the required time.

Therefore, knowing the parameters of the degree completion time line along with instances of time extensions serve as valuable information to know regarding the degree program and institution requirements for degree completion.

THREE

Finding a Research Problem

Sometimes, a research team you are invited to join hands a research problem to you: "We've been studying degree completion rates; you'll be working on attrition of undergraduate students who have just finished their freshmen year." Sometimes you know exactly what you want to study: "I want to know why some senior college students demonstrate 'senioritis.'" Often, however, you will have either no idea as to what you want to study—or you will have too many ideas. This chapter will help you zero in on a good research problem.

This book distinguishes between three related terms. The term *research topic* is used here to denote a general area of study. Here are some topics to illustrate this use: learning styles, school-to-work transition, class size, charter schools, and curriculum alignment. A *research problem* is a more narrowly defined issue that represents only one aspect of the research topic, such as "Problems encountered by first-year teachers."

The *problem statement* is the carefully worded research issue as it appears in the dissertation. It is even narrower than the research problem. As explained in later chapters, problem statements may be formulated in several different ways. Here is one form that a "state-mandated testing" research problem might take as a problem statement: What problems did career teachers experience with the testing program?

In general, you would move from a research topic to a research problem and then to a problem statement, as the following discussion explains. However, you may be able to take a shortcut, moving from a research problem to a problem statement. Although there will be much individual variation in the way this process is executed, you should find the following method useful for moving systematically from topic to research problem. Later chapters explain a process for defining the problem statement.

MAKE A PERSONAL ASSESSMENT OF TOPICS

You probably have some topics in mind that you have been considering. No one coming to the end of a degree program has a blank mind. You begin, therefore, by making your own preliminary assessment of the topics you have been mulling over.

Use a form similar to the one shown in Exhibit 3.1 to complete this assessment. Most students will find it helpful to rate three topics. Assessing only one or two may narrow your perspective prematurely; assessing more than three may get too complicated. Rate each topic on the basis of each criterion and then compute the total. Keep in mind that you are making only a preliminary assessment, not a final decision. The eight criteria are discussed below.

Professional Significance

What constitutes professional significance? There are no simple benchmarks. Only a scholar steeped in the literature of a given field can make a final judgment. One

Exhibit 3.1 Assessing Your Topics

Criteria	Topic 1	Topic 2	Topic 3
Professional significance			
Continuing professional interest			
Personal interest			
Career advancement			
Knowledge, experience, skills			
Likely support			
Time required			
Accessibility			
Total score			

CODE: 5, excellent; 4, very good; 3, good; 2, fair; 1, poor

way to take a rough measure of significance, however, is to ask yourself, "How will it play in Dubuque?" You imagine a colleague in Dubuque, Iowa, who reads an abstract of your study. Will that colleague be interested? Or you imagine yourself being introduced to an audience of your colleagues. The introducer says, "It gives me great pleasure to introduce Doctor X, who has just completed a study of . . ." Do you feel embarrassment or pride?

There are, of course, other more objective ways to assess professional significance. A professionally significant study makes an important contribution to the field in one of the following ways: it tests a theory; it contributes to the development of theory; it extends existing knowledge; it changes prevailing beliefs; it suggests relationships between phenomena; it extends a research methodology or instrument; or it provides greater depth of knowledge about previously studied phenomena.

Often, of course, significance inheres not in the topic area itself but in the way it is examined. Consider these examples.

NOT PROFESSIONALLY SIGNIFICANT:

What resources are available for the study of career education literature for young adults? The topic lacks significance because several excellent and current lists already exist.

PROFESSIONALLY SIGNIFICANT:

What career paths are conveyed in the juvenile literature recommended by librarians? The topic has potential significance because research on it is likely to add to existing knowledge.

Note that the criterion speaks of significance, not originality. Some students worry unduly about trying to find a topic that has not been studied before or fret because "someone has stolen my topic." In a scientific sense, all topics are original; the replication of previous studies is a crucial part of scientific investigation. Consider this example. You are interested in principals' decision-making processes. You have tentatively identified four principals. You discover that another student wants to study the decision-making processes of those same principals. You have several ways of resolving the seeming conflict: use different instruments and methods; find different principals; or explore different aspects of decision making.

Continuing Professional Interest

The second professional criterion involves the extent to which the topic will continue to be of interest to the profession in general. The implication is that you should avoid studying educational fads—unless the study focuses on the nature of educational faddism. The hope is that you will do a study that will have value beyond the time when you receive your degree.

Consider, for example, outcomes-based education (OBE). Although this restructuring initiative embodied some useful ideas and was popular for a brief time, the controversy surrounding some of its value-laden ideas resulted in heated controversies that contributed to its demise. A study of its implementation would be of little interest at the present time. On the other hand, a study of federal- and state-mandated testing programs is likely to have continuing interest, since the problem is one that will not soon go away.

Personal Interest

Since you will be devoting a considerable amount of time to the study, obviously you should choose one that has great interest for you. Keep in mind, however, that doing the dissertation may be a way of awakening new interests.

Career Advancement

You also need to weigh the impact of your dissertation topic on your present and future career. There are three ways to view this issue.

1. If you plan to remain for an extended period of time with your present employer, then one of the main considerations is the immediate value of the topic to that employer. Therefore, you should consult with your superiors to find a topic that they believe will help the organization. For example, if your school system is experiencing continuing problems with violence in the schools, your superintendent may see a dissertation on the topic as a valuable contribution.

2. If you hope to take a leadership position in another organization and be able to consult, then the primary issue is the professional timeliness of the topic. Timeliness in this case means that it will be of great professional interest during the foreseeable future. Obviously it is difficult to predict educational

trends, but you can make some reasonable assumptions about what will continue to interest educators.

3. If you hope to find a position in higher education, then the major issue to consider is its professional power. Will the topic impress search committees, enable you to publish a few articles and a book, and provide a launchpad for a research career? In essence you ask this question: "Will this topic resonate in higher education?"

Professional Knowledge, Experience, and Skills

You can probably do the best job of researching a topic if it draws from your professional knowledge and experience and uses your research skills. For example, if you have been teaching in a nontraditional schedule for several years and believe you have found a way to make it work, that experience and knowledge would simplify your investigation.

Likely Support

The more support you have, the easier it will be to complete the dissertation. The most important source of support is your committee chair. If he or she is actively involved in researching a topic that you have chosen, then obviously you can anticipate a close working relationship. In addition, as explained in Chapter 1, you might also consider whether a particular topic is likely to receive foundation or government support.

Time Required

Although time is more a factor of method than topic, you should be sure that the topic is sufficiently narrow so that it can be intensively studied within a reasonable time.

At the stage of finding a topic, many students think too ambitiously, planning a study that sounds as if it might take two or three dissertations. One student, for example, talked about his topic in this way: "I'd like to research what improves student writing." The topic is simply too broad since the factors are so complex, involving writing ability, the writing curriculum, writing instruction, and teacher and peer feedback.

Accessibility

For all studies there are issues of access. Will the school board approve of your study? Will school administrators cooperate? Does your study require parent and student approval? Will teachers be willing to answer questionnaires or be interviewed? Such issues need to be considered carefully.

CONDUCT A BROAD SCAN OF THE LITERATURE

With your three possible dissertation topics assessed on a preliminary basis, you should next conduct a broad scan of the literature. A broad scan is the first of a three-phase review of the literature that you should undertake. Many students believe that the review of the literature occurs in one intensive period of reading. It makes more sense to see it as a continuing process. As Exhibit 3.2 indicates, each of the phases has a different purpose, and each makes a contribution to your knowledge base.

The discussion here is concerned with the broad scan. The next chapter explains the focused review; Chapter 8 examines the comprehensive critique.

Your goal for the broad scan is to increase your knowledge so that you are better able to make a final decision about the research topic and the research problem. How much time you spend on this step will depend on the time

Exhibit 3.2 Three Phases of the Literature Review

Phase	Chief Sources	Purpose
Broad scan	Reviews of the literature	To assist the researcher in identifying a research problem
Focused review	ERIC	To develop a proposal prospectus and research proposal
Comprehensive critique	All sources	To provide a scholarly foundation for the study

available, your existing knowledge, the resources available to you, and how many topics you investigate. You have a choice about this last issue. If the preliminary assessment has convinced you that one topic is clearly superior, then investigate only that. If you feel torn between two of the topics, then you should investigate both. And if you have ample time available and feel very confused, then review all three possible topics.

Organize for the Broad Scan

As you conduct the broad scan, organize your work, keeping in mind the following guidelines.

1. Begin to keep a research journal. The research journal is your personal record of your ideas, feelings, and actions as they relate to your dissertation. The journal will provide a very useful source as you do your dissertation and reflect about your progress. Here is a sample entry to illustrate how you might use the journal:

   4/23. Read a good article in the Review of Educational Research on "School to work transitions for youth with disabilities," by L. Allen Phelps and Cheryl Hanley-Maxwell (67, 197–226). That might make a good topic; I could do a follow-up study of students with disabilities.

2. Develop a good filing system. You should see your filing system as a flexible one that changes as your study takes shape. You should develop a system that reflects your own way of organizing materials. You should also investigate software that makes it possible for you to computerize your knowledge base. At this stage of searching for a topic, you probably will have one general folder for each topic you are investigating. As explained in the next chapter, once you have identified a topic, you will reorganize your files, setting up a folder for each major phase of the problem you have decided to study.

3. Secure the approved style manual. Check with the chair of your department to determine which style manual is to be followed. Get a copy and follow it precisely. If you have a choice, purchase and use the current edition of the *Publication Manual of the American Psychological Association* (usually referred to as "APA"). Published by the American Psychological Association, it is the style manual most widely used in education.

4. Hold on to useful sources. Whenever possible, make copies of articles, chapters in books, and shorter monographs. Do not rely on your note-taking skills. If the entire book seems useful, purchase your own copy if it is still in print. If you cannot buy the book, copy the title page and pages that seem especially useful.

5. Get full bibliographic information. Style manuals vary considerably in relation to the information they require in endnotes and reference lists; check the manual

you are using to determine which information is needed. However, err on the side of completeness. For example, the current edition of the APA manual requires you to use the author's first and middle initials in the reference list, not the author's first name. However, you may decide to submit your article to a journal that requires you to include the first name; you, therefore, should have it in your files so that you do not have to look it up again.

6. Begin your search record. You should find a search record helpful to you throughout the dissertation process. A search record is what the term implies: a detailed account of the search process you used. Exhibit 3.3 shows one useful form. The search record will help you be more systematic about your search. It can also provide the data you need for your literature review chapter, and it will enable your chair to give you constructive feedback about your search process.

Read to Inquire

At this stage, your chief purpose in retrieving and reading sources is to help you make a final decision about the topic and frame the research question. As you read, keep several questions in mind and note the answers as they become apparent to you.

- Which specific issues have been most often studied? Which seem to warrant further research?
- Which authors and which studies are most often cited?
- What instruments are available?
- Which methods are frequently used?
- When were the major studies completed? Does the number of research studies seem to be increasing or decreasing?
- Which theories are used as a foundation?

This last question perhaps requires an extended comment. A theory is a set of related concepts, assumptions, and generalizations that systematically describe and explain behavior in educational organizations (Hoy & Miskel, 1987). For example, Janis and Mann (1977) developed a highly respected theory of conflict in decision making that has been used as the basis for several studies. Theories can suggest problems. For example, you might design a study that would measure how principals use what Janis and Mann describe as "defensive avoidance." The use of theory is discussed further throughout this book.

Concentrate on Research Reviews

One of the best ways to conduct the broad scan is to concentrate on research reviews. A research review is a scholarly article on a topic (such as promotion and retention) that reviews the major research studies about that topic to give readers a broad picture of what is known. Research reviews are usually written by eminent scholars

Exhibit 3.3 Search Record

Date of Search	Topic	Purpose	Database, Descriptors	Time Period	Results
10/4 trial	Teacher development	Find methods	ERIC staff development; careers; development	1980–present	Found five essential sources

in the field who retrieve all the sources available, evaluate the research, select the most reliable research studies, and synthesize what is known.

As you search for research reviews, also look for the term *meta-analysis.* A meta-analysis is a research review that uses complex statistical processes to determine overall effects of a given intervention. There are several ways to find research reviews and meta-analyses.

- Check the library catalog to see if the library has any books whose titles begin with the words *Handbook of Research*. Such handbooks have been published for most of the major fields of education. For example, the *Handbook of Research on Teaching the English Language Arts* (Flood, Jensen, Lapp, & Squire, 1991) is an excellent source of reviews on that subject; its only limitation is that it does not include sources published after 1990.
- Look for a series of books titled *Review of Research in Education*. A new volume is published each year, containing reviews of several topics. For example, Volume 22 (Apple, 1997) contained excellent reviews of research in the following areas: educational politics and policy, race and education, and teaching and research.
- Review current and back issues of the journal *Review of Educational Research*. This journal is devoted to publishing such reviews; each issue contains reviews of several topics.
- Use the library's computerized databases to search for research reviews. The most important database in the field of education is Educational Resources Information Center (ERIC). You may have some difficulty finding and using ERIC, since its funding was reduced in 2003. At the time of this writing, it could be accessed at the Educator's Reference Desk,

http://www.eric.ed.gov. If you have difficulty finding and using ERIC, check with the reference librarian at any university library. The database PsycLIT is useful for any topics related to the field of psychology. In using ERIC at this stage, you may find it helpful to limit your search by using the descriptor literature review, along with the descriptor that identifies the topic. The "literature review" descriptor identifies any source that includes a review of the research. This is the way the search would be designated for literature reviews of the topic "teacher motivation": SS motivation AND teachers AND DT=literature review. That command tells the computer to search for both terms (motivation, teachers) and to limit the search to the document type "literature review." (Further details about searching ERIC are available from a reference librarian.)

- Also check the Internet. At this stage, the Internet can help you in several ways. You can use it to search ERIC and other databases. You can review course syllabi and reading lists from many university professors. You can use e-mail to contact others who are doing research in one of the topics you are considering. And you can participate in forums or discussion groups organized around one of your topics. In using the Internet, keep in mind that most of the material provided has not been screened or evaluated.

Obviously you may use other sources if you have the time. Some students find it helpful at this stage to read dissertations on the topic. Sources for dissertations include *Dissertation Abstracts* and *ProQuest,* now available via the Internet. In addition to reviewing the literature and explaining the methodology, many dissertations conclude with a section titled "Recommendations for Further Study."

REFLECT AND DISCUSS

With this preliminary knowledge base established, you are now prepared to discuss with faculty, students, and colleagues the one or two topics you are considering. Your intent here is not to let others make your decision but to get objective input about the topic. This is what you might say to a faculty member:

> Could you spare about half an hour to help me focus on a dissertation topic? I have some tentative ideas, and I know your feedback would be useful. My preliminary reading has convinced me that it would be helpful to investigate the career development of lateral entry teachers. Does that topic in general make sense to you?

You would then proceed to structure the dialog so that you get the objective views of your partner about the most important of the criteria listed in Exhibit 3.1.

FIX ON THE RESEARCH TOPIC AND RESEARCH PROBLEM

You have made your own preliminary assessment. You have completed the broad scan, developing your knowledge base. You have also gotten input from objective sources. All those data should enable you to select a research topic. Once you have settled on a research topic, you are then ready to identify the research problem. As Exhibit 3.4 indicates, the research problem is only one of many possible approaches to a research topic; the research problem may be considered one "slice" of the topic "pie."

If you have difficulty moving from topic to problem, apply these questions to the topic you have in mind. They may suggest some profitable angles for you to explore.

Exhibit 3.4 Examples of Research Topics and Problems

Research Topic	Possible Research Problem
Violence in schools	Causes of student-to-student violence
Curriculum alignment	Curriculum alignment and its effect on teacher planning
School to work	Community support for school-to-work programs
Writing feedback	Effects of peer feedback on quality of writing
Performance	Problems in scoring performance assessment

- What causes it?
- Who is especially involved in it?
- When does it occur?
- What effects does it have?
- What types are there?
- How do various groups perceive it?
- At what stages does it occur?
- What will make it better?
- What makes it effective?
- What relationship does it have to other phenomena?

You can use that statement of the research problem in several of the next steps you take in the dissertation process.

TECHNOLOGY TECHNIQUE: UNIVERSITY RESEARCH LIBRARIANS

Dissertating students often overlook the university librarians as the students tend to depend upon the Internet. These librarians are available to assist students in the search for available resources pertaining to the topic of interest, and they are trained to assist dissertating students with the process. Their assistance is available upon request—take advantage of this resource!

To take full advantage of this service, graduate students should obtain background information on the potential topic. In other words, they should do some research and have some idea as to what is available. Before telephoning or e-mailing the reference department at the university library to schedule an appointment, the graduate student should prepare a list of questions to be asked concerning (a) available databases, (b) appropriate procedures to be followed in requesting materials, and (c) assistance that can be provided by the university librarians.

At the time of the scheduled appointment with the university reference librarian, arrive on time. Be prepared to describe your research topic—talk intelligently about the topic—and have available in either electronic or hard copy format resources that you have already consulted. Ask the reference librarian to help select appropriate databases to continue your literature search and review. Do not expect the university librarians to do your work; however, they are willing to assist. Remember the results will be only as good as the information you provide.

FOUR

Conducting a Focused Review of the Literature

With the research problem identified, you should next conduct a focused review of the literature. Whereas the broad scan helped you identify a research topic and problem, the focused review will help you develop a prospectus and a proposal. A *prospectus* is a preliminary outline of the proposal that will help your committee provide input for the proposal itself; the proposal is a research contract that details specifically for you and your committee the details of your research plan. Chapter 7 explains how to develop the prospectus; Chapter 10, the proposal:

REORGANIZE YOUR FILES

In identifying a research problem, you probably found it helpful to organize your files according to the topics you were investigating. In doing the focused review, you should organize your files by the divisions of the research problem you have chosen. Suppose, for example, that your research problem is "factors that influence the motivation of high school students to learn in learning communities." Based upon your reading, your knowledge of what the proposal will require, and your sense about the direction of your study, you might use these categories with respect to the research problem:

- Theories or conceptual frameworks of motivation to learn
- Research methods in studying motivation to learn
- General findings with respect to motivation to learn
- Motivation to learn specific subjects
- Factors affecting motivation to learn
- Motivation to learn for high school students in traditional learning environments
- Motivation to learn for high school students in smaller learning communities

As you continue to review the literature, you will find it helpful to review your filing system and reorganize it as needed. At this stage, you should see your files as an evolving set of documents.

RETRIEVE ALL RELATED ABSTRACTS

The next step in the process is to retrieve all the sources that seem to be useful and are available. The easiest way to accomplish this step is through a computerized search of the databases available on the Internet or through your university library. For the comprehensive critique in the dissertation, you will need to consider all available resources; however, for the prospectus and proposal, a search of computerized databases should suffice. More than likely, the one you will find most useful is ERIC—the world's largest digital library of education literature (http://www.eric.ed .gov), since it collects sources in the field of education. If your research problem involves a psychological aspect, you might also find the PsycLIT database useful, since it focuses on psychology. Both ERIC and PsycLIT, for example, include sources on motivation.

The discussion that follows provides some general guidelines for doing an online search. The technology is changing so rapidly, however, that you should check with a reference librarian for current specific suggestions for doing a computerized search.

In getting ready to use one of these databases, you should find its thesaurus helpful. In information retrieval, the thesaurus is a catalog of the terms (called *descriptors*) used to search the database. The thesaurus also identifies other search limitations, such as type of document, educational level, and years covered. Check with the librarian for help using the thesaurus and to determine which years are available in print and which years are available electronically. Or access ERIC by visiting http://www.eric.ed.gov.

Use the appropriate descriptors to search the database, using an "abstract" format. Information specialists use three terms in specifying format. *Bibliographic information* gives you author, title, date of publication, and other identifying information about the source. *Abstract* adds a summary of the contents, written by the author of the report. *Full text* is the complete text—the entire paper or article. At this stage, you should find abstracts most useful.

If you encounter any problems using the computerized database, confer with a reference librarian, who can advise you about search strategies. In addition to accessing computerized databases, you should also locate and retrieve any sources listed in the research reviews that look promising. Keep in mind that at this stage you are trying to identify the major sources so that you are well informed about the research on your topic. You are not trying to capture every reference.

EVALUATE THE RESULTS

Now you need to evaluate the results of your search, since much of what you have retrieved will not be of use. The following guidelines should be useful here.

1. Check the author. If you recognize the author's name from your previous reading, the source is likely to be important. For example, any report by Henry Peel on leadership is likely to be useful, since he is considered one of the leading authorities in the field.

2. Check the title. If the title suggests that the article is a report of practice, the article will be less useful. Contrast these two titles: "Block Scheduling as a Motivation Tool in the Secondary School!" and "Student Performance in Block Scheduled Smaller Learning Communities Classes." The first does not sound too useful; the title implies that it is an enthusiastic report of one school's experience written by one of the faculty—a practioner's report. The second sounds like a research report. At this stage of your reading, concentrate on research studies, not reports of practice. However, both research and practice reports may be of value for the completed document.

3. Check the date. Generally, unless you are conducting a historical review, you should give more weight to recent studies. Here's a rough rule of thumb: for the prospectus and the proposal, emphasize the most recent 10 years.

4. Note the source. In general, give greater consideration to journals that publish research reports and reviews. Give less consideration to periodicals read chiefly by practitioners. For example, *Business Education Forum* is a fine periodical for practitioners,

usually including articles that report on one school's experience. It tends not to publish research reports. On the other hand, the *Delta Pi Epsilon Journal* usually includes research reports. This latter journal is also a refereed journal, meaning that all articles must be approved by experts in the field before they are published. Usually, research articles in refereed journals will be most useful. Check with a periodicals librarian who can help you determine if a given periodical is refereed.

5. Check the document type. You should give the highest priority to sources identified as information analyses. These terms are also used to identify research reports: research review, review of the research, meta-analysis, and a review of the literature.

6. Read the abstract. The abstract should give you a good idea about the potential usefulness of the source.

Based upon your analysis of these factors, code each source with one of three numbers as follows.

1. This is a "must-have" source; it is on-target and sounds very useful.

2. This is a "maybe" source; it might be helpful and should be checked if I have the time and need additional sources.

3. This is a "no" source; it is not useful at all.

Check for Prior Dissertations

This is also a good time to determine if any dissertations have been completed on your topic. Use a database termed *ProQuest Dissertations & Theses*. If that database indicates that someone in another university has already completed a dissertation on your topic, confer with the librarian to determine how you can secure a copy. Do not despair if you find one or more dissertations have already been completed on a topic you have chosen. You can always find ways of making your dissertation sufficiently distinct. A dissertation topic cannot be covered by a copyright.

RETRIEVE THE FULL TEXTS OF THE MOST USEFUL SOURCES

With these evaluations made, you should then retrieve the full text of all useful sources. Begin by retrieving the full text of your #1 sources. Regardless, be certain to obtain relevant bibliographic information, because the information may be needed later. One suggestion is to photocopy the title page of the source, and on that page, record the name of the publication, the volume and issue number, and the appropriate page numbers. By doing so, time will be saved as the date of the final defense approaches. Here is some general advice about retrieving full text.

Books: Buy them if in print, borrow them from the library, or use interlibrary loan. The Internet lists all libraries whose catalogs are searchable on the Internet.

Chapters in Books: Copy the chapter.

Dissertations: You can borrow the dissertation from the library of the university conferring the degree. Or you may order it by accessing http://www.proquest.com/en-US/support/contact.

Journal Articles: In doing an ERIC search, you will note at the top a document number. Some are preceded with the symbol *ED;* others, with *EJ.* The ED denotes that the source is a research document available on microfiche. Most research libraries contain all the fiches produced by ERIC and the equipment necessary to read and print from the fiche. The symbol EJ indicates that the source is an article from a journal. You will need to consult the journal for the full text of EJ sources. An increasing number of research reports are available in full text by using the computer. Check with a reference librarian for current information.

If you find that you do not have enough #1 sources for your prospectus, then move to the #2 sources. A very rough rule of thumb is to have between 15 and 20 sources for the prospectus and from 25 to 50 for the proposal and the dissertation. However, keep in mind that the author of the dissertation needs to be "all knowing" about the research topic. Therefore, the number of needed sources is likely to vary based on the dissertation topic and research problem. Be sure to keep all the sources and your evaluations. You may find it necessary to retrieve those you have rated "2," and you might even reconsider the "3"s. Also be sure to update your search record and continue to keep your journal.

USE PRIMARY SOURCES

At this stage and all succeeding stages in the dissertation process, keep in mind a crucial distinction between primary and secondary sources. A primary source is the original report; a secondary source is an article that refers to the primary source.

To illustrate the difference, consider these examples. Shore conducts a study on motivation and reports the results in a journal article. The Shore report is a primary source. Pate publishes a review of the research on motivation in which he cites the Shore report; in this situation the Pate article is a secondary source. Good researchers do not rely on a secondary source; they search for and retrieve the primary source. Secondary sources may sometimes distort the findings of the primary source, and they do not provide sufficient detail.

DEVELOP AN ANNOTATED BIBLIOGRAPHY

At this stage, you should find it helpful to develop an annotated bibliography. Check with your dissertation adviser to determine if he or she has any special requirements for the annotated bibliography. Following are the elements usually included.

- An explanation of the search and retrieval process you used, including the database searched, the descriptors used, the publication dates, and other limiters
- Complete listing of the bibliographical information, using the latest edition of the APA style manual and listed alphabetically
- A brief summary and evaluation of the source

Exhibit 4.1 shows one item in an annotated bibliography.

Exhibit 4.1   Example of Annotated Bibliography

TOPIC: Teacher Certification

DATABASE SEARCHED: ERIC

DESCRIPTORS USED: Teacher Certification

YEARS SEARCHED: 2000–present

Simpkins, Jim. (2011). What does Washington State get for its investment in bonuses for board certified teachers? Schools in crisis: Making ends meet. ED 517748; Center on Reinventing Public Education, University of Washington.

Approximately $100 million will be spent by Washington State to fund bonuses for teachers who receive national board certification. The intent of the investment is to improve the state's teaching force and encourage the most capable teachers to work in high-poverty schools. Does it accomplish those goals? Includes extensive bibliography. Good summary—but limited. USEFULNESS SCORE: 2

A CONCLUDING NOTE

The focused review should require from 10 to 20 hours at the computer. You should find that time a good investment, since it will move you forward in the preliminary steps of writing a winning dissertation.

TECHNOLOGY TECHNIQUE: SOFTWARE FOR MAINTAINING REFERENCE INFORMATION

There are many ways you can accomplish storing, retrieving, and coding your reference information. Techniques may range from a very simplistic approach to a more complex approach. A simplistic method of maintaining a reference list may involve the use of an Excel spreadsheet. The spreadsheet may include reference information as discussed in this chapter. This information may be sorted and/or filtered using the tools within Excel to retrieve and categorize the reference information in a manner useful to your literature review. You may choose to use a more sophisticated approach, which may involve software programs such as Ref Works, Cite Like, or Zotero, just to name a few; many others exist and provide a wonderful resource for managing your literature review. Software programs, such as the three aforementioned, provide you with a tool to store, manage, and retrieve your references in a manner that allows you the capability to maintain your literature review in a more methodical and organized fashion.

Regardless of whether you decide on a more simplistic or complex approach for maintaining your literature review, choosing a system that works for you will allow you ease of access, retrieval, and categorization of thoughts, ideas, and concepts related to your study.

Making a Preliminary Choice of Methodology

With a clear idea about your research problem and a sound knowledge of the related literature, your next step should be to make a preliminary choice of methodology. In doing so, you should distinguish between three related concepts: *research perspectives, research types,* and *research methods.* This chapter will provide only an overview of these concepts and suggest how to make a preliminary choice of methodology. You will need to consult with a faculty member who specializes in research design and methods to be sure that your methodology is sound. Chapter 9 provides additional detail about explicating the methodology for the proposal; Chapter 16, for the dissertation.

QUANTITATIVE AND QUALITATIVE PERSPECTIVES

A research perspective, as used here, is a general view and use of research approaches and methods. There are two major perspectives: *quantitative* and *qualitative.* The quantitative perspective derives from a positivist epistemology, which holds that there is an objective reality that can be expressed numerically. As a consequence, the quantitative perspective emphasizes studies that are experimental in nature, emphasize measurement, and search for relationships. If a study uses language such as the following, it probably has used a quantitative perspective: *variable, controls, validity, reliability, hypothesis, statistically significant.*

On the other hand, a qualitative perspective emphasizes a phenomenological view in which reality inheres in the perceptions of individuals. Studies deriving from this perspective focus on meaning and understanding and take place in naturally occurring situations (McMillan, 2012). If a study uses language such as the following, it probably has used a qualitative perspective: *naturalistic, field study, case study, context, situational, constructivism, meaning, multiple realities.*

Mixed Method Perspective

Although some researchers seem chiefly concerned with the differences between the two approaches, Creswell (2009) and Morgan (1997) explain how the two perspectives can be combined. Four general ways of combining the two were identified by them, based upon two factors: which one is primary and which secondary, and which one is used first and which second.

1. Quantitative primary, qualitative first. The researcher begins with a qualitative approach as the secondary method, using the qualitative data as a basis for collecting and interpreting the quantitative data (the primary method).

2. Quantitative primary, quantitative first. The researcher begins with a quantitative approach as the primary method, using qualitative follow-up to evaluate and interpret the quantitative results.

3. Qualitative primary, quantitative first. The researcher begins by collecting quantitative preliminary data as a basis for collecting and interpreting the primary qualitative data.

4. Qualitative primary, qualitative first. The researcher begins with the primary qualitative data, using quantitative follow-up to interpret the qualitative data.

Project-Based Studies

Project-based dissertations are an emerging trend as it permits students to use current practice as the basis for research; the project is usually designed to evaluate the practice—research—for effectiveness. For this type of study, some universities permit students to work together as groups to complete the research; however, the framework for the research must be grounded by research theory. Typically, the first part of the study is spent observing the practice, while the second component is to conduct a detailed evaluation of the practice and its effectiveness in reaching the intended outcomes. Be cautious when considering this type of dissertation, because many graduate faculties may not be familiar with this type of study, and those faculties may not think that the final product is a dissertation.

RESEARCH TYPES

The term *research type* is used here to identify the general research approach. Although authorities in the field seem to differ as to how the types of research are classified, the following approaches, which are most often used in educational research, represent some of the options available to you as a researcher. To simplify the discussion, they are divided into whether they tend to use a quantitative or a qualitative perspective, although there is much overlapping in many of the types.

Studies Primarily Quantitative in Nature

The following types of research are primarily quantitative in nature.

Experimental Research

Experimental research uses methods originally applied in the physical and biological sciences. In most experiments, the following procedures are used: a sample of subjects is selected, they are assigned randomly to experimental and control groups, and a treatment is administered to the experimental group only. The two groups are then evaluated on the basis of the dependent variable and the consequence of the independent variable. The latter is the presumed cause of the dependent variable.

Here is an example of an experimental design. The researcher randomly assigns 200 fourth graders to 10 classrooms. Five of those classes are randomly selected. They are given a new program on ethics; the other five classes are given no program at all. At the end of the school year, both groups are administered a measure that assesses their attitudes about and knowledge of ethics. Statistical techniques are used to analyze the results.

Quasi-experimental Research

A quasi-experimental design is one that follows the general procedures of experimental research, without the use of a control group or without random assignment, since random assignment or the use of control groups is often not feasible in educational settings. In a quasi-experimental study of ethics, the researcher would not use random assignment but could use one of several strategies to compensate for its absence. The researcher might, for example, administer a pretest to all students, provide the treatment to half of the students, administer a posttest, and use a statistical procedure known as the *analysis of covariance* to determine if the treatment made a difference.

Causal-Comparative Research

Causal-comparative studies are designed to determine the possible causes of a phenomenon. Sometimes these studies are called *ex post facto research* since the causes are usually studied after they have had an effect upon another variable. For example, a study which examines the effects of grade retention uses a causal-comparative design by studying the effects of not being promoted when comparing the later performance of those who were retained and those who were promoted.

Correlational Research

Correlation studies are designed to analyze the relationships between two or more variables, ordinarily through the use of correlation coefficients. You might, for example, study the type of licensure held by teachers and student achievement to determine if there are any statistically significant relationships between these two factors. Keep in mind the caution that correlation is not causation. Correlational studies may show a direct relationship between two factors but cannot prove causation.

Descriptive Research

As the term implies, the purpose of *descriptive research* is to describe a phenomenon. Although some professors deprecate descriptive studies, these studies can be especially valuable as one of the early stages in a research project. Descriptive studies report frequencies, averages, and percentages. For example, you might study the attitudes of teachers in public schools toward the superintendent and the local governing board. You would not draw any conclusions about relationships, but only report frequencies, averages, and percentages.

Evaluation Research

Evaluation research makes judgments about the merit or worth of educational programs, products, and organizations. It is typically undertaken to aid administrators in making professional decisions. Evaluation studies are usually described as either *formative* or *summative*. Formative studies are made while a new program or product is being developed; summative studies, when it has been completed. You might do an evaluation of a testing program required by the *No Child Left Behind* legislation, performing both a formative and a summative assessment.

Studies Primarily Qualitative in Nature

The following types of research tend to take a qualitative perspective.

Case Study Research

A very useful definition of the case study is that provided by Yin (2009): "A case study is an empirical inquiry that investigates a contemporary phenomenon in depth and within its real-life context, especially when the boundaries between phenomenon and context are not clearly evident" (p. 18). Although, as Yin and others state, case studies often use quantitative measures, they more often tend to take a qualitative perspective, concerned with exploring, describing, and explaining a phenomenon. You might undertake a case study of a new consolidated high school in its first year of operation.

Ethnographic Research

Ethnographic research is a special type of case study research. It is distinguished from other types of case studies because it uses the theories and methods of anthropology to study the culture of schools and classrooms. For example, you might do an ethnographic study of the educational background and employment experiences of female school administrators to use in curriculum planning for preparing female administrators.

Action Research

Most action research documents how an educational problem was identified, understood, and solved by practitioners. For example, you might document how you and your colleagues resolved the problem of student "texting" during class at the elementary, middle, and secondary school levels.

There are, of course, other methods employed in educational research, such as philosophical research, historical research, and legal research. Each of these has its own characteristics and uses special methods.

RESEARCH METHODS

Research methods, as the term is used here, are the specific techniques used to collect data with respect to the research problem. Five methods are typically used in educational research.

1. Tests and Measurements. Tests are administered and measurements made to determine the extent of change.

2. Interviews. Interviews are conducted with individuals or groups to ascertain their perceptions.

3. Observations. Observations are made to determine what is occurring and what individuals are doing.

Exhibit 5.1 Relationship of Types and Methods

Type/Method	Test, Measurement	Interview	Observation	Survey	Document
Experimental	P		A		A
Quasi-experimental	P		A		A
Causal comparison	P		A		A
Correlational	P		A		A
Descriptive	A	A		P	A
Evaluation	P	A	A	A	A
Ethnographic		A	P		A
Action		A	P	A	
Case study		A	P	A	A

CODE: P, primary method used; A, additional method that may be used.

4. Surveys. Surveys are administered to assess opinions, perceptions, and attitudes.

5. Documents. Documents are analyzed to establish the record.

As Exhibit 5.1 indicates on the preceding page, the types of research explained above make more use of certain methods than they do of others, although there is much variation in the relationship of types and methods.

MAKE PRELIMINARY CHOICES

The process explained here assumes that in developing the prospectus you will make only a preliminary choice that may be modified through discussion with your committee. When making a preliminary choice regarding the research methodology, the type of study, and data collection methods, weigh the following factors.

1. The nature of the research problem. This is probably the most important factor of all. In fact, the identification of the problem and the choice of methodology may be seen as interactive processes, with each influencing the other. For example, if you are concerned with identifying a possible causal relationship between parents' reading to children in the home and children's interest in reading, the study would obviously call for a causal-comparative study.

2. Your research skills. Although it is always possible to develop new skills, you will find that designing and completing the study will be easier if you have mastered the required skills. If you do not understand advanced statistics, you probably should not undertake a quasi-experimental study.

3. The research skills of your committee. As will be explained later, it is essential that at least one of your committee has expertise in the methodology you have chosen.

4. Your career plans. If you aspire to a career in higher education, you might be wiser to use one of the quantitative types or a mixed-research design, since many university faculty members are still biased in favor of quantitative studies. However, more and more prospective dissertation committee members are becoming well versed in qualitative research design.

5. The time available. In general, qualitative studies take more time than quantitative ones. Ethnographic studies are extremely time intensive.

6. Access to the research site. In general, school administrators will not grant access for experimental studies since parents are reluctant to have their children participate in any experiment, regardless of its promise.

TECHNOLOGY TECHNIQUE: DATA ANALYSIS SOFTWARE I

As you consider the various research methodologies and designs, you need to consider the type of data to be collected and the process and procedures that will be used to analyze the collected data. Data analysis software is available for both qualitative and quantitative studies. Please keep in mind that any collected data must be in computer readable form before any analyses can occur.

Quantitative data are much easier than qualitative data to analyze as the analysis or analyses can be completed quickly using statistical data analysis software. The challenging aspect of quantitative data is preparing the data for analysis as the collected data will need to be "computerized" in some form. Previously, a data entry operator would key the data; however, today's technology allows the scanning of such data into computer readable form. Examples of quantitative microcomputer data analysis packages are Statistical Analysis Software (SAS), Statistical Package for the Social Sciences (SPSS), SysStat, and MiniTab.

Qualitative data are more challenging to analyze as the data are not numerical but text, or words. As a part of the analysis process, the words are to be coded in a format that is computer recognizable. For the data to be correctly coded, the same person must code all the data. If it is not feasible for one person to code the data, then a review process needs to be implemented. The review process, which is a verification of the coding, requires another individual or individuals to review what has been coded to ascertain that all individuals involved perceive and interpret the data in the same manner. NVivo is the leading qualitative data analysis software, and many universities have the software available for faculty and graduate students.

Dissertating students should take advantage of technology when analyzing data. Regardless of the type of research conducted, data analysis software should be used to streamline the analysis process.

SIX

Organizing and Scheduling Your Work

Throughout this book you will find specific recommendations for organizing and scheduling several aspects of the dissertation project. This chapter suggests a general planning strategy that many graduate students have found helpful.

Before examining the specific suggestions about scheduling your work, you should understand the importance of realistic scheduling. As you make planning decisions, be realistic about how much time you will need. It is better to set reasonable deadlines and meet them than to set unrealistic ones that have to be changed again and again.

What is a realistic amount of time to schedule for the project, from proposal to defense? Obviously the answer will depend upon a number of factors—such as the methodology chosen, the response time of the chair, your professional and personal commitments, and your own work habits. In general, most students will find that 12 to 16 months is sufficient for completing the research and the writing. Rather than depending upon such estimates, however, it makes more sense to develop a schedule that reflects your best judgments about your pace.

DEVELOP A PLANNING CHART

Begin by constructing a large chart similar to the one shown in Exhibit 6.1. The size of the chart will depend upon the space available, the length of time you will need to complete the dissertation, and the size of each entry. In general, a long narrow chart about 18 to 48 inches should be best. Label five horizontal rows, as follows:

Administration. In this row you will be noting all the important administrative requirements and actions, such as formally organizing the committee. Be sure to note the examinations you must take. Exhibit 6.2 shows the typical sequence of required actions. Be sure to check the current university catalog.

Course Work. In this row you will note which courses you need to complete and when you plan to complete them.

Literature Review. You will note in this row the three phases of the literature retrieval you will complete for the prospectus (the broad scan), the proposal (the focused review), and the dissertation (the comprehensive critique). You will show in this row when you begin and complete each phase.

Writing. You will enter here when you expect to complete the writing of the prospectus, the proposal, and the dissertation. In scheduling the dissertation writing, note when you think you will be working on each chapter, ordinarily allowing one month for each.

Research. You will note here when you will begin and conclude the research. Chapter 11 explains the major

Exhibit 6.1 Sample Planning Chart

STRAND	6/3–16	6/17–30	7/1–14	7/15–28
Administration				
Course work				
Literature review				
Writing				
Research				

methodological steps used in most educational research; Chapter 16 explains how to implement the research plan. Review Chapters 11 and 16 for the details you should enter in the chart; then divide the chart into several narrow columns, each column marked with a two-week time span. If you think you can finish in one year from the time you start planning, you will need twenty-six columns; if you think you will need eighteen months, then you will need about thirty-eight columns. That gives you a planning chart on which you enter all the important dates as they relate to the five aspects that need to be planned.

MAKE THE TENTATIVE ENTRIES

With the chart laid out, you can now make the tentative entries. Turn first to the aspect of "administration." This is where you will schedule all the administrative steps you have to take and the institutional deadlines you have to meet—such as selecting a chair, scheduling a proposal hearing, submitting your study for approval, and registering for graduation. It seems to work best if you start this part of the planning by beginning at the end. You should, therefore, decide tentatively when you would like to defend your dissertation. This is the key date that will affect all others. Consider how much time you will need to do the research

Exhibit 6.2 Completing Your Program: Steps in Sequence

The following steps are typical ones for completing a graduate degree. Check your university catalog for requirements and dates.	
1. Take any qualifying examinations.	Usually after completing 9–18 preliminary semester hours of course work
2. Complete course work.	At your pace—limited by university regulations
3. Pass comprehensive exams.	During or after last term of course work
4. Select dissertation committee.	When you are ready to begin serious work on dissertation
5. Hold prospectus conference.	Any time mutually convenient for student and committee
6. Hold proposal defense.	When committee approves; draft to committee two weeks prior to defense
7. Submit Institutional Review Board (IRB) approval.	Following prospectus approval and prior to collecting data
8. Hold dissertation defense.	When all members of committee approve; they should receive defense draft at least two weeks prior to defense
9. Apply for graduation.	Usually three to four months prior to graduation date of institution
10. Submit approved dissertation to graduate school, dean, department chair, and dissertation chair.	Usually three or four weeks prior to graduation
11. Submit IRB closure form.	Usually completed immediately following submission to the graduate school for final approval

and write the dissertation, and determine when you can most likely graduate. Then check university policies and calendars for the deadline for defenses, being sure to allow yourself some slippage. Thus, if you want to receive your doctorate in the May commencement and the university deadline for the defense of dissertations is three weeks prior, tentatively aim for a dissertation defense in the first week of April. Enter that notation in the appropriate cell.

With this key date established, you can now tentatively plan for the rest of the administration steps. Ordinarily you will include the items shown in Exhibit 6.2. Also note any major examinations you must pass. Check the university catalog for the important deadlines.

Obviously the entries you make in this administration row will be influenced by the policies and calendars of your own institution and your own preferences for the amount of detail you include in a planning chart. Just remember to block in all the key meetings, deadlines, and forms to be filed.

Now complete the "course work" strand by noting all the courses you still must take and when you will complete them. Then turn to the "literature review." Indicate when you will start or have started the broad scan; then note when you have finished or will finish it. Do the same for the focused review and the comprehensive critique.

Now turn to the "writing" strand. In this strand you enter all the dates for writing the prospectus, the proposal, and the dissertation chapters and for submitting manuscript to your chair and the committee. Again it makes sense to do some backward planning, setting the final target first. Check your entry for the dissertation defense and decide when you should submit to your chair what you hope is the final revision of the last chapter. Ordinarily this should occur no later than seven or eight weeks prior to the date for the defense.

Here is the rationale for such a time lag: (a) Your chair needs two weeks to read the final revision; (b) your chair needs a few days to notify you and the other committee members that the final chapter is now approved and the defense can go forward; (c) you or the person you have hired to do your word processing needs two weeks to make final changes in the entire dissertation; (d) you need one week to prepare copies of the dissertation for your committee; and (e) your committee should have at least two weeks to read the dissertation before the defense. Obviously this time period can be reduced by putting more pressure on yourself and your committee, but increasing the pressure at the end is a foolish thing to do. You become harried, and your committee feels annoyed. With that final writing target established, tentatively block in the rest of the writing deadlines, allowing yourself ample time to revise and revise again. In making these writing entries, remember that you do not have to write the chapters in the sequence in which they will appear in the dissertation. Some students prefer to get a quick start on the research and write the "results" chapter as soon as the data have been analyzed; they then write the "methodology" chapter, then the earlier chapters, and then the final chapter. Check with your chair to see if he or she has any preferences about this matter.

Now block in the important steps in the "research" strand, beginning with when you will identify the research topic and research problem. Then note when you will decide about the methodology. The other steps you enter will depend upon the methodology you have chosen. Again, allow yourself ample time and provide for some slippage.

Finally, step back and review the whole chart. Ask yourself these questions:

1. Have I entered all important university deadlines?

2. Have I allowed ample time for the chair and the committee to read chapters?

3. Have I provided for slippage and delays?

4. Have I planned realistically, allowing myself some breaks?

5. Have I taken into account any special demands of my employer that will affect my schedule?

6. Are the strands of the chart coordinated—do they dovetail with each other in a synergistic fashion?

Once you have revised your planning schedule, you should review it with your chair, who can give you some helpful input based upon his or her experience in working with other students and other dissertation committees.

Technology Technique: Chart Software

Creating and maintaining a chart of events within your planned time line is crucial to helping you focus on the end result—the successful completion of your study. There is no one way, or correct way, to create this chart. This technique is very personalized to what way works best for you. For example, some students outline their time line in their yearly calendar by placing monthly actions that will "pop up" at a specified date to serve as reminders that the specific item is due. This type of visual is a constant reminder to the student of due dates and item(s) that are due to whom. Another example is to create a time line of due dates and place tasks in chronological order by due date.

Either strategy may be effective. The purpose is to find a method that works best for you by keeping you moving forward toward the completion of the study.

SEVEN

Developing the Prospectus and Organizing the Committee

The prospectus is a general sketch of your research plan, submitted to your committee before you develop the formal proposal. This chapter provides a rationale for developing a prospectus, explains how to develop it, and suggests how it can be used in organizing the committee.

PROSPECTUS RATIONALE

The prospectus provides a preliminary and tentative overview of your research problem and the methodology. See Exhibit 7.1 for an example of a prospectus.

Although many students do not bother with a prospectus, experience suggests that it is a very useful step in the process. First, it enables you to bring together and systematize all the preliminary work you have done so far. More important, it enables your committee to give

Exhibit 7.1 Example of Prospectus

Mario Gutierrez   October 15, 2005

PROSPECTUS: DOCTORAL DISSERTATION

Topic: Performance assessments

Research problem: What problems do social studies teachers encounter in using performance assessments in the classroom?

Methodology:

RESEARCH PERSPECTIVE: Qualitative primary, qualitative first

RESEARCH TYPE: Case study

RESEARCH METHODS: The research will make primary use of observations, supplemented by interviews. Three teachers of American history will be observed during class sessions when they have decided to use performance assessments. Each teacher will be interviewed after the observation. The research will cover only the second term of the school year.

Time Line

Plans call for the dissertation to be defended in April 2006. A detailed but tentative planning calendar is attached.

---

you substantive input with respect to your problem and methodology before you write the formal proposal. Many students have spent months developing a proposal, only to find that the committee had different ideas about the problem or the methodology.

PROSPECTUS DEVELOPMENT

The prospectus usually includes three elements:

1. Research topic and research problem

2. Methodology

3. Preliminary calendar for completing the dissertation

COMMITTEE SELECTION

Since the procedures of forming a committee and the policies regarding committee composition vary so much from school to school, you should know and follow your school's procedures and policies. However, there is a general process that has been found to be effective, regardless of specific procedural differences. At the outset, it might be useful to discuss the timing of the committee selection process as it relates to the development of the prospectus and the proposal. In most instances, you will find that this is the optimal sequence: develop the prospectus; organize the committee, using the prospectus; then develop the proposal, using committee input. Here again the procedures of your school will influence how you handle this matter.

There are some good reasons for getting the committee organized before you develop the proposal. The proposal is a detailed research plan, and the chair should play an active role in its development. The chair's help and support at this stage can make a crucial difference. In too many cases, students come to a professor with a detailed proposal that they have spent months working on and ask the professor to chair the committee. The professor says, "Yes, I'll agree to serve, but I'll want you to make several major changes in the proposal." Or in an even worse eventuality, the professor responds, "No, I don't want to direct any research that I have not designed."

Thus, early in the process you should choose your chair—and do so before inviting other committee members. The chair plays the most important role and should have a say about the composition of the rest of the committee. D'Andrea (1997) discovered that 80.1 percent of the dissertation chairs surveyed indicated that they wished to be consulted on the makeup of the committee. In 2012, the lack of structure in the dissertation process, which is likely impacted by the standards established by the dissertation director or chair, continues to be a problem (http://www.niu.edu/csdc/coach ing/theses_dissertations.shtml).

It might be helpful at this stage to jot down the names of three professors who are likely candidates and then rate them as your first, second, and third choice. In evaluating the faculty you are considering for chair, you can use the following criteria.

Availability. Will that professor be available during the period you will be doing your research and writing the dissertation? Here you consider not only the professor's reputation for being available for conferences but also the professor's academic plans. Is he or she coming up for a tenure or promotion review? If so, how will the review process and the ultimate decision affect availability? Is the professor planning a sabbatical? Is the professor close to retirement?

Reputation for Responding Promptly and Constructively. Some professors are notorious for delaying students inordinately. They sit on chapters for weeks without reading them. They demand needless and excessive revision. They change their minds often about what they expect in a chapter. Steer clear of such individuals. On the other hand, also avoid the professor who is considered too easy. Do not invite one who has low standards, who returns chapters without having read them carefully, who wants to process students instead of educating them as researchers. With such an individual, you may finish faster, but your work won't have the quality it would have with a more demanding chair.

Interest in Your Research Topic. Your progress will be facilitated if your chair has a genuine and strong interest in what you are researching. The chair is more likely to devote special time and effort to dissertations on a topic that he or she considers important and relevant.

Interpersonal Compatibility. All other things being equal, it makes sense to work with a chair to whom you can relate. You will be working together for a year or more, and there is no point in working with someone who does not have much respect for you or is unreasonably impatient with your idiosyncrasies.

Research Skills. You want to be sure that at least one person on your committee has depth in the methodology you selected. If possible, choose a chair who has that depth. If the professor you are considering for chair meets all other criteria except this one, then you probably should invite him or her to serve, knowing that you can find the methodological expertise in another committee member.

Complementarity. Does the chair complement you in important ways—can he or she give you what you need? In a sense, this may be the most important criterion. The student researcher and the dissertation chair are like a team in many respects: What the student lacks, the chair should be able to supply. As you think of yourself as a student researcher, what do you need most from your chair? Research know-how? Access to subjects? Help with your writing? Emotional support? Professional credibility?

With your three choices ranked, you should now contact your first choice. The best way of making this contact is probably to write the professor a letter in which you indicate your interest in having him or her serve as chair, enclose the prospectus, and note that you will be calling to make an appointment to discuss the issue further. If your first choice turns you down, go to your second, and then your third choice. If you get turned down by three professors, then confer with the chairperson of the department to ask for assistance in finding someone to sponsor your research.

COMMITTEE DYNAMICS

Once you have resolved the issue of chair, you should give your attention to the composition of the rest of the committee. Make a preliminary list of faculty members you think you might want to invite, but do not contact them until you have conferred with your chair. In making this preliminary list, consider these factors:

- You want at least one committee member who complements the chair regarding expertise. If your chair does not have the research depth you need, then be sure one of your committee does.
- You want committee members who are generally available and who will provide the assistance you need when you need it.
- You want a committee whose members can get along with each other; you do not want to be caught in interfaculty crossfire.

With some names tentatively in mind, you are now ready for your first conference with the chair. This first conference with the chair should be purely an exploratory one. You do not want to resolve too many issues until the full committee has been constituted. Therefore, any initial discussion of the research problem or the methodology should be tentative and open-ended.

However, you do want to get the chairperson's input about the makeup of the committee. Some members of the faculty are simply unable to work together on dissertation committees, and the chair should be able to indicate his or her preferences. You should therefore deal with the subject with a comment like this: "Do you have any preferences about the makeup of the rest of the committee? I've been thinking about asking Professors X and Y to serve, but I would like your input."

At this initial conference, you should also explore in a tactful and sensitive manner the nature of the research relationship. There are four possibilities here. First, you will essentially carry out a piece of your chair's research. The professor will determine the specific nature of the topic and the details of the methodology. You will do the work, but the professor will call the shots and get the credit. If any publications come out of the research, your chair will appear as author and simply acknowledge your contributions. Second, you and the chair will work cooperatively as colleagues. You will collaborate actively throughout all stages of the research and will probably coauthor any publications emanating from the research. Third, you will play the major role throughout the research, but the chair will take an active interest in all phases. The final possibility is that it will be your show all the way. The chair will help you finish, but do not expect much substantive help.

Obviously, you can't ask about this relationship matter directly, but you do have to probe tactfully to be sure you both understand the research relationship.

Once you and the chair have reached a tentative agreement on the research relationship and the makeup of the committee, you should approach the other individuals you plan to invite. Again, write a letter and enclose the prospectus. The letter should say something like this:

> I would like to invite you to serve as a member of my dissertation committee. Both Professor X, who has agreed to serve as chair, and I believe that you could make a most important contribution. I am enclosing a prospectus that describes generally the research I propose to undertake.

That statement indicates to the faculty member being invited that the chair is on board and has discussed with you the composition of the committee. With the committee organized, you will have reached a significant milestone on your way to the dissertation.

TECHNOLOGY TECHNIQUE: TELECOMMUNICATION AND SOFTWARE EDITING TOOLS

The increase in technology has, in some ways, made it easier to schedule meetings that are interactive and provide face-to-face environments for both students and professors. These technological advances utilize "real-time" interaction for the student and committee members by providing an avenue to engage in conversations without physically sitting in the same room. This type of interaction allows for students to continue advancing toward the successful completion of their study by easing the potential conflicts of schedules.

Telecommunication: Skype for Teleconferencing. The use of Skype for conferencing and/or committee meetings (excluding the proposal defense and final defense) can be a useful technology tool to support the dissertation process. Often, when trying to schedule dissertation committee meetings, finding a time when all committee members are available can be most difficult. Given this, Skype may be useful as a means of conducting such a meeting. However, you should ask your committee chair how he or she feels about the use of Skype as a meeting technique prior to suggesting this for a meeting. Knowing how your committee chair feels about this type of meeting arrangement will provide you with insight as to the acceptability of conducting meetings using this format.

One of the great things about Skype is that it may be downloaded as free software, so there is no money involved. You simply access the Skype website, select the download button, and wait several minutes for the software to download. The program will notify you once the download is complete. The telephone calls have excellent sound quality and are highly secure with end-to-end encryption.

Skype software also offers users upgraded features if you have the need for additional Skype time and the advanced features. However, based on experiences, the free download will suffice and meet the needs of most situations (Parson, 2012). All you need to begin using Skype are the following:

- A PC or Mac computer
- An internet connection—broadband is best
- Speakers and a microphone—built-in or separate
- A webcam to make video calls

Hardware. The hardware specifications are pretty generic, but the software does require relatively new hardware components. To adequately run Skype on a Windows-based computer, the following are required: (1) a 1 GHz or faster processor, and (2) at least 256 MB of RAM. The Skype program supports Windows XP, Windows Vista, and Windows 7. To adequately run Skype on a Macintosh computer with OS X 10.5 or 10.6, the following is required: (1) a 1 GHz or faster processor, and (2) 1 GB of RAM. The Skype program also works on many types of Linux; its requirements are (1) a 1 GHz or faster processor, and (2) 256 MB of RAM.

Software. Often the Skype software runs autonomously without your computer system prompting you to download additional software so the Skype program may run; however, it does depend on some other software products. Windows-based computers must have DirectX version 9 or above currently installed. The DirectX usually comes preinstalled with Windows. On a Macintosh computer, you need to update QuickTime to its latest version for Skype to work properly. To utilize Skype on a Linux-based machine, the system needs the Pulse Audio, ALSA, and OSS software.

Special Equipment. To utilize the Skype program, you will need the capability to hear and transmit audio. Computers such as laptops that have built-in speakers and microphones do not need any add-on accessories; however, the sound quality may not be as good as a dedicated headset. Therefore, the purchase of such devices may increase the quality of the experience.

Computers without a built-in microphone require one to be attached externally, either as part of a headset or on its own. Additionally, video calls over Skype require a webcam. Any available webcam model that is compatible with the computer system will suffice. Our experience has been that the newer built-in computer webcams have a much better quality than previous computer models. You should view the computer's webcam for quality; if the quality does not measure up to your standard, then an external webcam should be purchased.

Software Compatibility. Making sure your computer system's software is compatible with your dissertation chair and committee members' is often an overlooked part of the process. Discussing and testing the capability of each member's computer may save you a lot of time and frustration during the writing and feedback phase of the process.

E-mail Submission of Documents. Before you begin submitting parts of the dissertation to your committee (either chair or other committee members), a simple test of submitting a document would be in your best interest as a means of ascertaining if documents may be accessed. It is also important for you to be able to access documents sent by your committee chair and committee members. If capability problems exist, go ahead and make arrangements to either upgrade your computer and/or software or make other arrangements so that you and your committee may communicate electronically with access to all documents.

Editing Tools. Most editing tools are compatible with current computer hardware and software. Generally speaking, most editing tools require the following specifications to adequately run the program:
Windows

- Microsoft Word 2000 and up
- Windows 98, ME, NT, 2000, and XP
- Internet Explorer 5.0 and up

Macintosh

- Microsoft Word for Mac 98 and up
- Mac OS X version 10.3 or later

Software Editing Tools. There exists a voluminous amount of editing tools to assist you with writing, if this is the direction you choose to take. The editing tools available for a graduate student provide different types of assistance. The tool may suggest possible alternatives to the sentence, or it may mark problem errors for later review. Regardless, it is a tool designed to help the student with formal writing of a thesis or dissertation. Most of these editing tools are valuable, but you are cautioned to consider the price of the tool, ease of use, and technical support. A simple Google search of editing tools will produce enough fodder for you to consider if one of the tools will meet your needs.

Additionally, the installed track changes function on your computer may be used to assist with the editing of the document. Each version of the document may be saved as a separate file, and then changes can be made to the document based on the feedback from the committee members. The importance of this type of system allows for you and the committee to refer to previous edit suggestions in case the need arises or questions arise regarding the need to delete and/or remove information.

One tool cannot be advocated over another. However, it is important to agree to a single method throughout the process. This improves the clarity and focus for you and the committee.

II

Developing and Defending the Proposal

Conducting a Comprehensive Critique of the Literature

Before explaining how to conduct a comprehensive critique of the literature, it would be useful to review the three types of literature review: the broad scan, the focused review, and the comprehensive critique. As explained previously, the broad scan relies chiefly on reviews of the literature to help you identify a research problem. The focused review chiefly uses ERIC to assist you in providing a knowledge base for your prospectus and the proposal. The comprehensive critique uses all available sources to locate any research that has a direct bearing on your research problem; it also involves the use of your critical judgment in assessing the quality of the research. When you write your proposal and the literature chapter in your dissertation, you will use relevant sources located in all three phases. Those identified in the comprehensive critique will probably be the most useful.

MAINTAIN GOOD RESEARCH PRACTICES THROUGHOUT THE SEARCH

As you conduct the comprehensive critique, be sure to keep in mind and apply sound research practices, as follows:

1. Maintain your search record. A current search record will help your chair and the reference librarians suggest additional sources.

2. Keep your research journal. Make entries that reflect your progress and your problems.

3. Make photocopies of all sources. In the comprehensive critique, you should rely on full-text, primary sources rather than on abstracted or secondary ones.

4. Be sure that the photocopy has full bibliographic information. Check all entries for accuracy.

5. Check the reference list of every source you have located. That reference list will give you additional leads to other sources.

6. If you store information in a computer file, back up all files.

7. Get expert help whenever you need it—from your committee, reference librarians, and other students.

8. Keep your dissertation chair informed about progress and problems.

You may also find it useful at this stage to set up and maintain a home page on the Internet so that others interested in your research problem can keep in touch with you.

DEVELOP A FOCUSED OUTLINE OF THE SEARCH

Before undertaking the comprehensive critique, you should develop an outline for the search. If you have already developed a topical filing system as suggested earlier, you should review it to be sure it reflects your current understanding of the literature relating to your research problem. You also should review the sources you have identified, as a way of noting the logical divisions of the problem. The search outline you develop should be sufficiently broad in scope to include all the issues that you will need to deal with in the literature chapter—but not be so broad that you sacrifice depth for coverage.

This latter point needs special emphasis. Many student researchers make the mistake of writing a review that is broad but superficial. If you read research reports in scholarly journals, you will notice that the review of the literature is narrowly focused, not broadly conceived. To clarify this matter, suppose you are doing a study on teacher leadership in curriculum. Here is an outline that is much too broad:

1. The definition of *leadership*

2. The nature of curriculum leadership

3. Leadership in site-based management models

4. The nature of teacher leadership

5. The history of teacher leadership

6. Teacher leadership in curriculum

7. Teacher leadership in other areas

The outline above includes so many topics that each issue would necessarily be treated briefly. Contrast that outline with this one that focuses directly on the topic.

1. Teacher curriculum leadership from a historical perspective

2. Teacher curriculum leadership in elementary schools

3. Teacher curriculum leadership in secondary schools

4. Teacher curriculum leadership and its relationship to curriculum quality

This matter of breadth and depth is so critical that you should consult with your dissertation chair.

One useful way to develop the first draft of the search outline includes three simple steps: First, list all the topics that might be covered, without worrying about the order. Then refine the list by eliminating those that seem peripheral and adding any that you might have overlooked. Finally, reorganize the refined list so that the order seems clear and logical.

Suppose, for example, that you have decided to study this research problem: secondary mathematics teachers' use of time in the extended period schedule. Here is the comprehensive list of topics you might generate in the first step:

1. Types of schedules, traditional and innovative

2. Effect of time on learning

3. How math teachers use time in the 45-minute period

4. How math teachers use time in the extended period

5. How math teachers plan

6. The effects of the extended period on student learning

7. The types of extended periods

8. Student attitudes toward the extended schedule

Here is a refined list of topics:

1. How math teachers use time in the 45-minute schedule

2. How math teachers use time in the extended period

3. Types of extended periods

4. Factors affecting math teachers' use of time

5. Effects of extended periods on achievement in mathematics

This is how the final outline might appear:

I. Factors affecting math teachers' use of time

II. Types of extended periods

III. Effects of extended periods on achievement in math

IV. How math teachers use time in the 45-minute schedule

V. How math teachers use time in the extended period

You can use the outline as a basis for reorganizing your files and for conducting the comprehensive critique.

ESTABLISH PARAMETERS FOR THE SEARCH

In consultation with your chair, define the parameters of your search. These are the issues to resolve:

1. Type of article. Should the search focus only on empirical research, or should it include as well other types, such as reports of practice and statements of opinion?

2. Language and national source. Should the search include only materials published in English? Should it include only research in the United States or other nations as well?

3. What time period should the search cover? In general, searches for theses and dissertations will usually cover the period from 1980 to the present. Historical studies, of course, cover a longer period of time. The topic itself might impose some time limitations. For example, you would probably not find articles on the extended period schedule before the mid-1980s.

4. Should the review include theories and conceptual frameworks? The review of the literature ordinarily should include a review of theories and concepts, but your committee may feel that they need not be included in your proposal.

CONDUCT A COMPREHENSIVE SEARCH

In conducting the comprehensive critique, remember that your goal is to locate all existing sources that relate to your research problem. Completeness is not important in the broad scan or the focused review, but it is for the comprehensive critique. The following discussion assumes that you have filed in an organized manner the results of your search of research reviews and of the ERIC database.

1. Use the Internet and commercial online services. The Internet can assist you in several ways. Many dissertations are now abstracted in the home page of the university where the degree was awarded. The Internet also gives you access to educational databases. Also, you can communicate with other researchers through online forums or discussion groups. Commercial online services provide many

of these sources but impose access and use charges, while the Internet is free except for connection charges.

2. Use other computerized sources. Check with the reference librarian in your university library to determine what other computerized data sources are available. Most research libraries include the following sources on CD-ROMs:

- Dissertations Abstracts. Most dissertations will be abstracted here. You will also find information about ordering dissertations.
- PsycLIT. As explained previously, PsycLIT is a database that includes research on topics in the field of psychology. Since many educational topics involve psychological issues, be sure to check this database. It has its own thesaurus, the *Thesaurus of Psychological Index Terms*. Using this thesaurus to identify search descriptors will greatly simplify the search process.
- Books in Print Plus. This database includes bibliographic information about all books still in print. You can look up your research topic in this reference.
- Essay and General Literature Index. This source will help you locate chapters in books, although it does not comprehensively cover the field of education.
- UnCover. This source provides the table of contents pages of nearly 17,000 journals, including most of those in the field of education; it is maintained by the Colorado Alliance of Research Libraries (CARL). It is a useful source for locating current publications that may not yet have been entered in the ERIC database.

3. Search for current conference papers. Papers presented at the annual conferences of such

organizations as the American Educational Research Association are often not entered into the ERIC database until a year or two after they were first presented. You should attend such conferences, being sure to get a conference program. If you cannot attend, order a copy of the program from the association. When you identify a paper that looks useful, write a letter such as the following to its author:

Please send me one copy of the paper on "Resilience in African American Males," which you presented at the 2005 conference of AERA. I could not attend your session, unfortunately. I am currently writing a dissertation on the topic and am sure that your paper will be most helpful in my own research. I would be happy to pay any charges involved.

Be sure to send a thank-you note if the author sends you a copy of the paper.

4. Read current journals. Each month you should make a regular check of journals in your field, especially those that often include research reports. Also read the newspaper *Education Week;* it usually includes very timely news about research reports just published.

CRITIQUE ALL SOURCES RETRIEVED

You have retrieved all the sources that seem to relate to your research problem. Now you should critique those sources to be sure that your review of the literature includes only sound research. The reader expects a critical review, not an indiscriminate collection. Although

Exhibit 8.1 Form for Evaluating Sources

Authors: _____Publication date: _____

Brief title: _____

Overall evaluation:

____ Sound in all respects

____ Generally sound, with some minor flaws

____ Seriously flawed

Research Problem: Research problem clearly stated; problem researchable.

Evaluation: _____

Comments:

Literature Review: Theory or conceptual framework presented; literature review comprehensive; literature review free of bias; studies summarized accurately and in sufficient detail; previous research synthesized, related to research reported.

Evaluation: _____

Comments:

Subjects: Clearly described; method of sampling described; selection free of bias; selection procedures appropriate; adequate number (usually at least a 60 percent response rate required for survey studies).

Evaluation: _____

Comments:

Instrumentation: Valid, with evidence for validity presented clearly; reliable, with evidence presented clearly; instruments described fully; administration procedures indicated; norms or standards specified; scores meaningful, without distortion; observers and interviewers trained and qualified.

Evaluation: _____

Comments:

(Continued)

(Continued)

Data Collection, Presentation, and Analysis: Data collection method described clearly, free of bias; data reduced appropriately; data presented clearly; data analysis clearly explained, supported by data presented.

Evaluation: _____

Comments:

Summary and Discussion: Summary accurate, sufficiently detailed, without distortion; findings interpreted appropriately; conclusions warranted by findings; interpretations clearly identified as such.

Evaluation: _____

Comments:

Criteria Specific to Research Type

EXPERIMENTAL AND QUASI-EXPERIMENTAL: Hypothesis clearly stated; direct manipulation of independent variable; design clearly explicated; extraneous variables controlled.

CAUSAL-COMPARATIVE: Causal condition previously occurred; extraneous variables controlled; differences between groups controlled; causal conclusions warranted.

CORRELATIONAL: Causation not inferred; size of correlation sufficient for use of results (group predictions require .40–.60; individual, .75).

DESCRIPTIVE: Conclusions about relationships not made; graphic representations accurate without distortion.

EVALUATION: Evaluation model identified; client and stakeholders specified; criteria specified; sources for criteria explained; standards clearly explicated, justified; evaluations rendered, supported with specific data.

CASE STUDY: Researcher's role identified; possible bias acknowledged, controlled; descriptions differentiated from interpretations; multiple methods of data collection and sources used; study of sufficient duration.

ACTION RESEARCH: Researcher's role identified; bias acknowledged; actions clearly described; actions evaluated, with adequate evaluation data provided; multiple perspectives and data sources used.

Evaluation on type-specific criteria: _____

Comments:

you can make some tentative judgments about research quality from an abstract, you can develop a valid critique only on the basis of a careful reading of the full text.

In undertaking that careful reading and keeping a record of the results, you should find the preceding form shown in Exhibit 8.1 to be useful. It was developed by reviewing several texts in research methods (McMillan, 2012, was especially helpful). Notice that it first lists criteria that apply to most research and then notes those criteria specific to a given type. Complete the form and then attach it to your copy of the source.

This careful critique of the research will enable you to make some important decisions as you prepare to write the literature review. What is the overall quality of the research on this topic? Which studies should receive major attention? Which studies are so flawed that they should be ignored? Which issues require further study?

A Concluding Note

Conducting a comprehensive critique will be an ongoing process throughout the dissertation project. Though time-consuming, it is an essential step that should not be hurried. Your goal is to know everything published so far on your research problem and to know which sources satisfy appropriate criteria. The knowledge you gain will help you write a sound proposal, write a quality literature chapter, and develop your own professional knowledge.

TECHNOLOGY TECHNIQUE: ELECTRONIC NOTE CARD

Information retrieved from the search may be organized using an electronic note card (see "Electronic Note Card," n.d.). There is nothing sacred about the design or format of the note card other than to say, design the note card so that the information may be stored and retrieved in whichever way works best for you. This technique is a quick guide to referencing information as you begin to develop themes, concepts, and ideas related to your literature review. Exhibit 8.2 is an example of the format of an electronic note card.

Exhibit 8.2   Electronic Note Card

Title:	Author:
Publisher:	City:
Date of publication:	Type of source:
E-mail address:	Date of download:

URL:
Research question:
APA citation
Direct quote
Research notes (in your own words)

Detailing the Methodology

Chapter 5 explained how you should make a preliminary choice of methodology and provided an overview of research perspectives, types, and methods. In this chapter, you will learn how to develop your methodology in detail. The chapter first explains the general nature of the research design and then more closely examines the research types and their related methods used most often in educational studies. (The discussion that follows draws from several sources: Cohen, Manion, & Morrison, 2007; Hubbard & Power, 2003; McMillan, 2012; Merriam, 2001; Schensul & LeCompte, 1999; Yin, 2009.)

THE RESEARCH DESIGN: ITS GENERAL NATURE

Regardless of the type of research you use, you should be certain to develop and use a sound research design. A research design is a specific plan or a recipe for studying the research problem. The following elements are commonly found in all research designs:

1. The research perspective. Indicate if the research is quantitative, qualitative, or mixed.

2. The type and subtype of the research. Identify the general type, as well as specify the subtype. For example, it is not enough to indicate that you will do a case study; you should also specify the subtype, such as ethnography.

3. The context for the study. Indicate where and when the study will be conducted and whether access has been assured.

4. The participants in the study. Identify who will be involved in the study, as in this example. "The study will focus on five southern female authors in the five southern states; they have all agreed to take part in the study."

5. The methods and instruments used to collect data. Explain how you will collect data—by document or archive examination, interviews, testing, observations, or surveys. Indicate the specific instruments, if any, that will be used. This example shows how the issue might be treated: Data will be collected by observations and interviews. The researcher will make weekly observations of the five southern authors and interview them in a focus group format.

6. Data analysis. Explain how you will organize, reduce, analyze, and display the data you have collected. Both quantitative and qualitative studies require an explication of how you will handle the data analysis. (For comprehensive treatments of data analysis, see Cohen et al., 2007, for quantitative studies, and Huberman & Miles, 2002, for qualitative research.)The value gained from qualitative research has generated considerable interest in this research methodology. Many institutions are now requiring that masters' theses and

doctoral dissertations contain both a quantitative and a qualitative component—which is called *mixed-method research*. In this approach, the qualitative component is used to verify or supplement the collected quantitative data.

THE RESEARCH DESIGN: TYPE-SPECIFIC ISSUES

Although the above features are common to all designs, they take quite different forms depending upon the research type. To aid you in explicating your methodology, each of the major types of educational research is noted in the following sections, with the specific questions you should answer. Ideas for quantitative and qualitative studies as well as mixed-method studies are provided.

Quantitative: Experimental and Quasi-experimental Research

As explained in Chapter 5, experimental research uses methods originally developed and applied in the natural sciences. Most experimental studies are intended to establish cause-and-effect relationships. Here is an example: Does accommodating the learning style preferences of elementary school students improve their mathematics ability? In quasi-experimental research, the researcher generally uses the same methods but cannot use random assignment of subjects to treatment groups. A quasi-experimental study might answer a question such as this one: "Does use of presentation software in teacher instructional delivery improve student performance on end-of-course or end-of-grade in selected courses?"

If you propose to undertake an experimental or quasi-experimental study, you should answer the following specific questions in addition to the general issues previously noted:

1. What subtype will be used? Most experts in research methods identify four subtypes, each of which differs in design details: single group, true experimental, nonequivalent groups, and factorial.

2. How will the subjects be selected? If random methods will be used, how will randomness be assured?

3. How will the subjects be assigned to experimental and control groups? If random assignment is planned, how will randomness be assured? If randomness is not planned, how will you deal with the problem that the groups will not be equivalent?

4. Will pretesting be used? If so, what test will be used?

5. What treatment will be applied to the experimental group? How long will the treatment last? What specifically will be done and by whom? How will you ensure that the treatment will be applied as intended?

6. How will the dependent variable be measured? Remember that the dependent variable is the likely result of the independent variable, introduced earlier in the study.

7. What inferential statistics will you use to establish relationships?

8. What methods will you use to control for threats to internal validity? Internal validity refers to the extent to which the researcher could claim that the independent variable caused the dependent variable. Research experts (Huck, 2012) have identified several threats to internal validity, such as the following: history, maturation, testing, and instrumentation.

9. What methods will you use to control threats to external validity? External validity is the extent to

which the findings can be legitimately generalized. Experts (Huck, 2012) have identified several threats to external validity, such as the Hawthorne effect, experimenter effect, novelty effect, and task effect.

Quantitative: Causal-Comparative Research

Like experimental and quasi-experimental research, causal comparative research (sometimes called ex post facto research) attempts to establish cause-and-effect relationships. However, the researcher has much less control over the independent variable and cannot use randomness in selection and assignment. For example, a researcher might use causal-comparative research to attempt to establish a causal relationship between students' home environments and performance on secondary end-of-course tests.

The methodology should answer the following specific questions:

1. What subtype will be used? Four subtypes are frequently used: between-group, time series, path model, and archival time series.

2. If between-group design is used, how will the homogeneity of groups be established? If a path model, what theory will be used as the basis? For archival time series, how will you control for history, maturation, and mortality?

3. In the interpretation of results, how will you avoid the post hoc fallacy—assuming that because one factor preceded another, it must have caused the other?

Quantitative: Correlational Research

Correlational studies attempt to understand patterns of relationships among variables. Although such studies cannot prove causation, they are useful in predicting one variable from another or building a theory about a complex phenomenon. Correlational research would be used to answer this question: "How are smartphone usage for required reading assignments and assignment submission related?"

In detailing the methodology, respond to the following issues:

1. What subtype will be used: bivariate correlations, multiple regression, discriminant analysis, partial correlations, or factor analysis?

2. How will the variables be measured? How will the validity and reliability of the measures be established? Why were these variables selected?

3. How will data be displayed? Will scatter plots or correlation matrices be used?

4. What correlation statistics will be used? Why were they chosen?

Quantitative: Descriptive Research

Descriptive research is used to describe the characteristics of a population by directly examining samples of that population. Descriptive studies make primary use of surveys, interviews, and observations. They are usually undertaken in the early stages of a phenomenon. Thus, a researcher might decide to use descriptive research to answer this question: "What are the distinguishing characteristics of teachers who seek National Board Teacher Licensure?"

These are the special questions to address, in addition to the general design issues previously noted:

1. How will the sample be selected—convenience, volunteer, quotas, or probability sampling?

2. What variables will be studied? Why were they selected?

3. If a survey will be used, what response rate will be required? How will you deal with the problem of nonresponse bias?

4. What statistics will be used to report results? How will data be displayed?

Evaluation

Evaluation research makes judgments about the merit or worth of educational programs, products, and organizations, usually undertaken to assist administrators in making professional decisions. Although evaluation is considered here as a type of research, many research experts distinguish between research and evaluation. For example, Cohen et al. (2007) note the features that they believe distinguish evaluation from research: Evaluation is parochial, in the sense that it focuses on a single entity; it examines multiple aspects of the unit being studied; it often originates with a client, not the researcher; and it is often undertaken when a decision must be made.

Of all these distinguishing features, the parochialism of evaluation seems to be the major obstacle in justifying it as research. Thus, a study is not likely to make a significant contribution to knowledge if it reaches a conclusion of this sort: "Instructional strategy is not effective." However, an evaluation study can escape the limits of parochialism if it accomplishes one or more of the following purposes:

- Provides an early test of a new approach or model of evaluation
- Develops an instrument that can be used in other studies
- Evaluates a program that is widely used but has had little systematic evaluation
- Documents how the evaluation results were used by groups of stakeholders

An evaluation methodology should address the following specific issues:

1. Who are the clients—who initiated the request for evaluation?

2. What evaluation model or theory will be used?

3. Who are the stakeholders? Who has an interest in the results?

4. What criteria will be used? How were they derived?

5. What standards will be used to make judgments?

Qualitative: Case Study and Ethnographic Research

Case study research is undertaken to provide a detailed description of a particular situation, organization, individual, or event. It is disciplined inquiry concerned with providing meaning by using inductive processes. As one type of case study, ethnography uses the methods and theories of anthropology to understand the culture of an organization. For example, you might undertake an ethnographic study of a charter school, delineating its purposes, values, norms, symbols, and celebrations.

Consider the following issues when explaining case study methodology:

1. What subtype will be used—ethnographic, historical, psychological, or sociological?

2. Will the study verify existing theory or generate new theory?

3. What community or intact group will be studied? Will the study focus on an individual, small work groups, single classroom, or school district?

4. What will be the role of the researcher? Many case study researchers identify themselves as "participant-observers."

5. If interviews will be used, what type—key informant, focus group, or life history?

6. How will the researcher provide for triangulation? Triangulation is used to mean a process of using multiple perspectives and data sources.

Mixed Method: Action Research

Action research is usually undertaken by a researcher who is deeply involved in the processes of identifying and solving an educational problem. Some action researchers study their own teaching or leadership processes. Others focus on colleagues or students. Many researchers attempt to solve problems in their organization by using action research.

Action research methodologies should deal with the following specific issues:

1. What is the goal of the action research?

2. What will be the focus of the action research?

3. What is the role of the researcher?

4. What procedures will probably be used to solve the problem?

5. What procedures will be used to document and evaluate the actions taken?

6. How will you guard against researcher bias?

DEVELOP YOUR RESEARCH DESIGN

One useful way of developing your research design is to begin by identifying the research perspective, as explained in Chapter 5. Then analyze your skills, the resources available, and the nature of the problem to decide tentatively about the research type. Use the input from the preproposal conference as well as the general and specific questions from the previous discussion to develop your research design. At that point in the process, you should consult with a faculty member who is known to be an expert in the research type you have selected. Ask the faculty member to critique your design; make the necessary revisions and additions. You will then be ready to explicate the details of the design in the proposal, as explained in the next chapter.

TECHNOLOGY TECHNIQUE: DATA ANALYSIS SOFTWARE II

Software for both quantitative and qualitative data analysis has been developed for both the mainframe computer and microcomputer. Discussion here is limited to microcomputer data analysis software. Specific software has been created for both quantitative and qualitative data analysis. For example, the Statistical Package for the Social Sciences (SPSS) has both mainframe and microcomputer versions as does Statistical Analysis Software (SAS). Yet spreadsheet software programs (i.e., Microsoft Excel) have the capability of generating descriptive and inferential statistics. Furthermore, similar software has been designed for qualitative research. For example, NVivo is one of the leading software packages for analyzing qualitative data. As with quantitative research, database programs (i.e., Microsoft Access) have the capability of analyzing qualitative data.

For both quantitative and qualitative data, various other statistical software programs are available. Yet the researcher needs to consider the expense of purchasing such software because it may be cost prohibitive. Before purchasing such software, the researcher should contact the university's computing support services office.Today, data analysis software, for both quantitative and qualitative data, may be available from such support services. The software may be available free of charge or at a reduced cost.

Regardless of the type of research (quantitative or qualitative) and/or the type of data analysis or analyses used, the credibility of the results—conclusions and generalizations—depend upon the accuracy of the data entry and data coding. When designing data collection instructions, the coding of the data for analysis is a very critical component.

TEN

Developing and Defending the Proposal

The development of the proposal is an exciting time. Once you are involved in this part of the research stage, you will think that the authors are somewhat disillusioned. But what we are saying is that this stage of the study is a time of exploration, receiving feedback, rethinking, and then determining the research path. All this is both exhilarating and exhausting. The development of the proposal is a continuous search to find the right ingredients to create a dynamic research study. Once you have "pulled" together all the ingredients, articulating your study to your research committee is crucial to conducting the research to reach conclusions, outcomes, and recommendations. Along the way, one resource that we often fail to utilize is our peers. Your peers can be of great help during the dissertation process. On the other hand, they can also be a hindrance as problems arise.

PEER COLLABORATION

Using peers to collaborate on various aspects of the research may serve as a beneficial resource to provide you with feedback on your study. Often we know what we want to do; the conceptual framework makes perfectly good sense to us as the "thinker." However, as we begin to articulate the study, or to synthesize the literature to others, the study becomes less clear, thus producing questions regarding the construct of the research. Therefore, taking the time to seek peer review and feedback regarding your work will enable you to continue focusing your research for clarity as well as provide the same assistance to others.

WEIGHING THE ADVANTAGES AND DISADVANTAGES

Using peer collaboration has both advantages and disadvantages. On the plus side, you and your peers can share the workload, dividing some of the tasks between you. You also get the benefit of an objective perspective. For example, a peer can see problems in your writing that you have missed because you are too close to your own writing. On the other hand, peer collaboration requires additional time. Moreover, interpersonal problems with your peers can add to your emotional stress. Review the matter carefully and ask your adviser for guidance about the issue.

STRUCTURING THE COLLABORATIVE

Your collaborative will probably be more productive if the group takes the time to specify the collaborative structure. Exhibit 10.1 is a form you can use for this purpose. The functions listed on the form will be analyzed briefly to ensure a common understanding.

Prepare for Comprehensive Examinations

Many collaboratives help members prepare for comprehensives. Members develop reading lists, discuss major works, identify likely questions, and share sample responses.

Exhibit 10.1 Developing a Structure for
Collaboration

1. List members, postal addresses, phone numbers, and e-mail addresses

2. Adviser

3. Convener for the collaborative

4. Are meetings anticipated? If so, note frequency and location.

5. Listed below are the functions by which peers can assist. Check all those that you wish your collaborative to provide.

_____ Prepare for comprehensive examinations
_____ Provide editorial feedback about writing style of chapters
_____ Assist with and contribute to literature review
_____ Assist with and contribute to data collection
_____ Assist with and contribute to data analysis
_____ Prepare for proposal defense
_____ Prepare for dissertation defense
_____ Develop an article for publication
_____ Provide emotional support

Adviser approval: _____Date _____

Provide Editorial Feedback

As the first draft of a given chapter is concluded, the group provides feedback on such issues as chapter organization, paragraphing, sentence structure, and word choice. These tasks are probably best accomplished by responding to written drafts, since most problems with the academic style are easier to spot in written form.

Assist With and Contribute to Literature Review

There are several ways the group can cooperate in completing a review of the literature. You can divide in relation to date of publication: Prior to 1950, 1951 to 2000, and 2001 to the present. You can also divide the topic.

For example, a study of teacher attitude toward account-ability might be divided in relation to these subtopics: attitude toward high-stakes testing, attitudes toward mandated curriculum, attitudes toward teacher incen-tives, and attitudes toward publicity about reform. In reviewing the literature on a controversial issue such as social promotion, two members might work on studies supporting social promotion, and two would concentrate on studies opposing social promotion.

Assist With and Contribute to Data Collection

Some collaborative groups have divided the data col-lection tasks. You can do this by site so that individual students collect data from three different research sites. You could also divide the tasks by collection method: one observes, one interviews, and one examines documents.

Assist With and Contribute to Data Analysis

Students who are strong in quantitative data analysis could focus on quantitative analysis. However, those with strength in qualitative methods would work on the qualita-tive results.

Prepare for and Contribute to Defenses

The collaborative groups can be of great assistance in helping members prepare for the proposal defense and the dissertation defense. The group could deal with the following topics: getting emotionally ready, organiz-ing the defense, using media to support the defense, handling difficult committee members and their ques-tions, and profiting from the defense.

Develop an Article for Publication

As Chapter 20 explains, you should give serious consid-eration to publishing from your dissertation. The collabora-tive group can be of great help here in planning, drafting, and submitting the article.

Provide Emotional Support

Most students seem to value the support received from a collaborative group. Completing a winning dissertation can be a very stressful experience, and a group of peers can support each other in dealing with a host of problems.

FORMALIZE THE STRUCTURE AND REQUEST ADVISER APPROVAL

Make a quick tally of individual preferences. Discuss those functions where the group seems divided. Summarize the results for members and the adviser, and get the adviser's written approval. The adviser's approval is critical, since collaborative structures challenge many academic norms.

HELP THE GROUP REMAIN PRODUCTIVE

Most peer groups develop predictable problems. The following suggestions should help the group solve these problems productively.

- Develop a meeting goal and agenda. You do not want the group to waste time and get off the topic. The best way to keep the group on task is to have a goal and an agenda. Keep this somewhat informal, such as this introduction:

  Tonight we will be helping each other develop an article for publication. Sue has agreed to give us some information she has collected on selecting a journal for publication. Then each of us will identify a publication we have tentatively chosen.

- Do a brief formative assessment after each meeting.

  So did we accomplish our goal?

- Conduct an interim summative assessment once every three or four meetings. Exhibit 10.2 (see p. 132) can be used to get members' perceptions.
- Deal with individual problems individually. Use peer pressure with members who are creating problems or not discharging their responsibilities. Identify the behavior, explain why it should be eliminated, and indicate the change you wish to see. Here is an example:

Sue, in the last two meetings, your comments have seemed very negative. Your negativity creates tensions among us. We value your input, but we hope you might speak more positively.

- Keep your adviser informed, but do not burden him or her with group problems.

Readers and Reviewers

Developing a peer review group to serve as readers and reviewers for your study is a useful resource that is sometimes overlooked. Hopefully, during your program of study, there has been a sense of professional learning community that has transpired among you and your classmates. This type of learning environment may be advantageous to all of you because you have been exposed to and learned how to read, interpret, and write research-based manuscripts. Therefore, a good use of resources at your disposal is to engage your classmates as reviewers of your study so that you may receive feedback from them on the clarity of your research. Talk with two to three of your classmates to ascertain their level of interest in this activity. This will also help each of you to continue strengthening your critical reading skills.

Exhibit 10.2   Interim Summative Feedback

DIRECTIONS

Read each statement below about your group. Then indicate to what extent you agree or disagree. Circle one of these choices.

SD   Strongly disagree
 D   Disagree
 A   Agree
SA   Strongly agree

OUR GROUP WAS . . .

1. productive, accomplishing our goals   SA   A   D   SD

2. cooperative, working well together   SA   A   D   SD

3. efficient, not wasting time   SA   A   D   SD

4. equitable, each person accountable   SA   A   D   SD

5. What was the group's strongest attribute?

_____

6. In what way could the group's performance have been improved?

_____

Miniproposal

The *miniproposal* may be a relatively new term associated with the thesis/dissertation process. But this activity may be extremely beneficial to you as you work toward a successful proposal and final defense of your study. The miniproposal is simply a mock-up of the real proposal defense. The miniproposal may be conducted as part of an assignment associated with a course, or as an activity that may be a part of your program of study. In either case, the miniproposal serves as a measure of how well you have conceptualized the study. The feedback you receive from the miniproposal can be used to strengthen your study as you move forward.

The makeup of the miniproposal may take on many forms. For example, some may only want the doctoral students associated with a specific cohort to engage in the miniproposal. Other miniproposal participants may include other doctoral students as well as faculty from the respective department or faculty from other departments and/or colleges within the institution. Regardless of the participants in the miniproposal activity, an important individual to include is your dissertation chair. This may serve as a valuable activity for your chair as well because he or she can also hear the feedback from other students and faculty regarding the strengths, areas of concern, and suggested improvements for your study.

As for when the miniproposal should be held, that is specific to each cohort of students and each institution. Generally speaking, the miniproposal should be held when approximately three-fourths of the total program of study has been completed by the student. This is in general terms and may vary depending on the program of study and sequencing of coursework and completed associated doctoral activities.

Developing the Proposal

If you have followed all the steps explained in the previous chapters, you should find it a relatively simple matter to develop and defend your proposal. If you have worked closely with your committee throughout these processes, there should be no anxiety at all about what might go wrong. This chapter, then, helps you tie together all those steps into a strong research proposal that you can defend without problems.

As you work on your proposal, keep in mind its importance. It is an implicit contract between you and the committee. You are expected to carry out the research as proposed, unless the committee approves changes you request. And the committee is expected to evaluate the dissertation on the extent to which you carried out your proposal. If, for example, your proposal did not specify the use of focus groups, a committee member should not criticize you at dissertation defense time for not using focus groups.

DEVELOPING THE PROPOSAL: THE BIG PICTURE

Although universities vary in their proposal requirements, almost all proposals include three major components: introduction to the study, review of the literature, and methodology. Observe that the overall organization of the proposal follows the conventional sequence of the first three dissertation chapters.

Two types of proposals are used in graduate research. The *comprehensive proposal* is a very detailed and full description of the proposed research. It essentially represents the first three chapters of your dissertation. The *working proposal* is a briefer form that has only enough detail to get you started in the research. To clarify the differences between the two, Exhibit 10.3 shows how the length of each section might vary in typical comprehensive and working proposals. Note a few major features of Exhibit 10.3. First, the working proposal is about one-third the length of the comprehensive proposal. Second, the two proposals include about the same amount of detail in the methodology section; the major differences between the two types of proposals are explained in Chapters 1 and 2.

Obviously it is essential for you in the early stages of developing your proposal to ascertain the committee's preferences about this issue. Some committees prefer the comprehensive proposal, since all the details are worked out before the research begins. Often a year or more is spent developing the comprehensive proposal; however, much less time is then devoted to completing the rest of the dissertation. Other committee members prefer to have the student use the working proposal, since they want the student to reduce the time developing the proposal and increase the time doing the research. The working proposal is more often used in qualitative research, since many qualitative studies use an emerging design, in which the methodology changes as the research moves along.

In writing either the comprehensive or the working proposal, remember to use the future tense, not the past tense, when referring to your study. The dissertation, on the other hand, uses past tense. Here are two examples:

PROPOSAL: Focus group interviews of ten teachers will be conducted.

DISSERTATION: Focus group interviews of ten teachers were conducted.

DEVELOPING THE PROPOSAL: WRITING CHAPTER 1

The first chapter of the proposal introduces the research proposal. In the full proposal, the first chapter usually

Exhibit 10.3 Length of Comprehensive and Working Proposals

Chapter	Comprehensive Page Length	Working Page Length
1. Introduction to the study	20	5
2. Review of the literature	40	5
3. Methodology	15	15
Appendix: Proposed time line	1	1
TOTAL	76	26

includes these elements: introduction to the chapter, the background of the study, the problem statement, and the professional significance of the study. The full proposal also may include the definitions of key terms and the delimitations of the study. The *delimitations* are the limitations you have imposed on the study that limit generalization. The working proposal usually includes in its first chapter the introduction, the problem statement, and the significance of the problem.

Introduction to the Chapter

The chapter begins with one or two paragraphs that serve only to get the reader into the chapter. The simplest way to accomplish this goal is to state the purpose of the proposed study. Here is an example:

This working proposal describes a proposed research study that will examine the nature of decision making in schools that have used site-based management for three years or more. This first chapter of the proposal introduces the study.

Background of the Study

The background presents to the reader the context for your study. Usually it explains what external factors might influence the study. In this sense, the "background" section says to the reader, "Here is what was happening in education that affected the study." For example, a 2005 study of how a district used curriculum standards to develop its curricula would probably be influenced by these background factors: the continuing concern for curriculum quality, the increased activity of the states in developing standards, and the expanded role of professional organizations in developing standards. Some committees also expect the discussion of the background to explain how your proposed study will contribute to the knowledge base.

In identifying the background factors, ask yourself these questions:

- What trends are occurring in this field?
- What new developments are most promising?
- What problems are surfacing in most schools?
- What societal developments are impacting the schools?
- If someone reads this proposal 25 years from now, what would the reader want to know about the background?
- What is the general state of knowledge about the research problem?

In most proposals, a discussion of three background factors would be sufficient. In the comprehensive proposal, each background factor you have identified would be explained fully in one page or more. The working proposal does not have to include an examination of the background unless the committee requires it.

The Problem Statement

As explained in Chapter 3 of this book, the problem statement is a very clear formulation of the research problem. Since the way the problem is stated will affect the organization of both the proposal and the dissertation, you should give special attention to its formulation. You have several choices about the way the problem is stated.

Hypotheses. Many problem statements include *hypotheses*. A hypothesis is the researcher's prediction or expectation of what the results will show. In research, hypotheses involve two or more variables, such as time on task and achievement. Hypotheses are derived from theory. As you review the literature about your research problem, you should look for theory-derived hypotheses. When the hypothesis is stated in a positive form, it is often termed a *research hypothesis.* Here are some examples of research hypotheses:

- There is a positive relationship between students' use of computers in learning mathematics and their achievement in mathematics.
- Students retained in first grade will have lower achievement in mathematics than those who are promoted.
- There is a positive relationship between first-grade students' achievement in reading and the time parents spend reading to them at home.

In experimental and quasi-experimental studies, the problem is often framed as a *null hypothesis.* A null hypothesis is a negative form of the hypothesis; it is a statement that the differences have occurred because of chance. The research study will determine if the null hypothesis is rejected or accepted. Here is an example of a null hypothesis:

There is no correlation between the extent of teachers' autonomy in developing curricula and students' achievement in science.

Research Question and Hypotheses. Many correlational and causal-comparative studies frame the problem statement as a research question followed by the research hypotheses. Here is an example:

RESEARCH QUESTION: Does teacher involvement in decision making affect teachers' morale?

RESEARCH HYPOTHESES:

1. Teacher involvement in decision making varies from school to school within a district.
2. Teacher involvement in decision making varies with decision-making content.

3. Teacher involvement in decision making affects morale in a positive direction only in certain schools and only with certain types of decision-making content.

General Purpose of the Study. Many case studies frame the problem statement as a general purpose. Since the case study typically uses an evolving design, the case study researcher is often reluctant to be overly specific at the proposal stage. Here is an example: "The purpose of this ethnographic study is to observe, describe, and analyze the culture of a charter school as it develops in its first year of operation."

The general purpose mode can also be used in action research, as in this example: "The purpose of this action research study is to plan, develop, and evaluate a conflict-resolution curriculum for students in a community college."

Single Question. Many qualitative studies frame the problem statement as an open-ended question. Here is an example: "In what ways do students use the Internet when they are working independently on the computer?"

General Question Followed by Two or More Specific Questions. To achieve greater specificity, the researcher may use an open-ended question supported by its related, more specific question. Here is an example from an evaluation study:

The general question this study will attempt to answer is this one: "Is the curriculum audit an effective and feasible tool for educational change?" That general question subsumes several related questions:

1. Is the audit feasible in terms of fiscal costs?

2. Is the audit feasible in terms of participant time?

3. Is the audit effective in the change process, from the perspective of administrators?

4. Is the audit effective in the change process, from the perspective of teachers?

In general, you should take the following steps in developing a clear and functional problem statement. First, identify a research topic. Read enough that you are able to refine the topic as a research problem. Then make a decision about the methodology. With the general method selected, decide what type of problem statement would be most appropriate. Throughout the process, check with your committee. Exhibit 10.4 indicates the typical relationships between type of research and type of problem statement.

Professional Significance of the Study

Both the working proposal and the comprehensive proposal should include a section explaining the professional significance of the study. This section in a sense answers these related questions: "Why is the proposed study worth doing?" and "What professional value will it have?" In this explanation, be sure that you do not speak to personal or local reasons, such as these:

- The district has adopted a new program.
- I was involved in the piloting of an extended period schedule.
- The school was moving to an interdisciplinary curriculum.

Instead you should speak to the contribution your study will make to professional knowledge. As explained in Chapter 3, a professionally significant study can contribute in one or more of these ways: test a theory, contribute to the development of theory, extend existing knowledge, change prevailing beliefs, suggest relationships between phenomena, extend a research methodology or instrument, or provide greater depth of knowledge about a previously studied phenomenon.

Exhibit 10.4 Research Types and Problem Statements

Research Type/ Problem Statement	Research Question and Hypothesis	Null Hypothesis	General Purpose	General Question	General Question and Specific Question
Experimental and quasi-experimental	Sometimes used	Usually used			
Causal-comparative	Sometimes used	Usually used			
Correlational	Sometimes used	Usually used			
Descriptive			Sometimes used	Sometimes used	Usually used
Evaluation			Sometimes used	Sometimes used	Usually used
Case study, ethnography			Usually used	Sometimes used	Sometimes used
Action			Usually used	Sometimes used	Sometimes used

Here is an example of how this issue of professional significance might be handled:

It is hoped that this proposed case study of differentiated supervision will make a contribution to the knowledge of alternative models of supervision. Though there have been many anecdotal reports from school districts using the differentiated model, such reports have relied primarily on surveys of administrators and teachers. Although several doctoral studies were conducted in the late 1970s, there have been no case studies reported in the literature since 1990. (For the earlier studies, see . . .)

The researcher would then continue to develop this line of reasoning, pointing out why additional case studies are needed.

Other Optional Components

As previously noted, some committees will require you to include in Chapter 1 of the proposal the delimitations and definitions. Check with your committee to determine if these are to be included.

DEVELOPING THE PROPOSAL: WRITING CHAPTER 2

In the typical proposal, Chapter 2 is the review of the literature. In the comprehensive proposal, the review of the literature is an in-depth synthesis of the knowledge base of your research problem. If you develop a comprehensive proposal, then in writing Chapter 2 of the dissertation, you need only update the proposal review. If you use the working proposal, then the synthesis can be much briefer, as will be explained. Both the working and the comprehensive proposal should review the theoretical and empirical literature.

Review the Theoretical Literature

Your proposal should include a review of the theoretical literature. The theoretical review should provide a basis for the empirical review that usually follows. You can accomplish this goal by reviewing the theories typically used in studying the problem you have identified or by developing a conceptual framework.

Review Theories

A theory is a series of concepts organized into assumptions and generalizations that lead to hypotheses about a phenomenon. Hoy and Miskel (1987) note several uses of theory: it guides research in a problem area, it facilitates understanding and analysis of complex phenomena, it aids practitioners in making decisions, and it provides a basis for predicting what might occur. For example, the Janis and Mann (1977) theory of conflict and decision making is useful in understanding under what conditions stress has a negative effect on the quality of decision making and when individuals use sound decision-making procedures to avoid making choices. The Janis-Mann theory has been tested in several studies of administrative decision making.

In the proposal you should review briefly the major theories related to your problem and then explicate in depth the one theory that you believe will be most useful in your own study. For example, a proposal to study decision making by a site-based management team might use this outline:

I. Review of theories of decision making

    1. Classical theories of decision making

    2. Administrative theories of decision making

    3. Incremental theories of decision making

II. Analysis of Janis-Mann conflict theory

1. Concepts

2. Assumptions

3. Generalizations

The review of theories in the comprehensive proposal might require about 10 pages. In the working proposal, a one-page list of the major theories and a one-page review of the theory you have selected should suffice.

Develop a Conceptual Framework. A conceptual framework is typically derived from theory. It identifies the concepts included in a complex phenomenon and shows their relationships. The relationships are often presented visually in a flow chart, web diagram, or other type of schematic. For example, Exhibit 10.5 shows a conceptual framework developed by the authors that explains what the teacher does in a particular class. The conceptual framework was developed by reviewing the extensive literature on the factors influencing teaching.

A careful reading of the literature should help you develop a conceptual framework. You should first identify the major concepts involved in the phenomenon. Then you should identify the more specific subconcepts related to the major ones. Next you should discern how the concepts and subconcepts are related. With that knowledge base established, you should experiment with several different visual representations of the concepts and their relationships. You should then choose a visual representation that will best show how the concepts and subconcepts are related. Finally, you should write a clear explanation of the visual representation. In the comprehensive proposal, the presentation and discussion of the conceptual framework might require five pages; in the working proposal, a one-page visual accompanied by one page of explanation should be sufficient.

Exhibit 10.5   Sample Conceptual Framework
Diagram

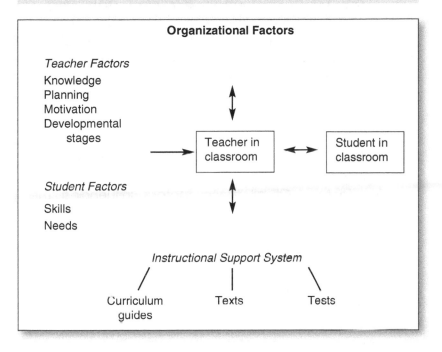

In developing your proposal, you should confer with your chair to determine if you should include either a review of theory or a conceptual framework—or both.

Review the Empirical Literature

The review of the empirical literature is an important part of the proposal. It is included in the proposal not simply to meet a traditional requirement but, more essentially, to link your proposed research with the prior research. As noted in Exhibit 10.3, the literature review of the working proposal is relatively brief compared with that of the comprehensive proposal. Regardless of length, both proposals should include the components discussed in this section.

Link the Review of the Literature With the Theoretical or Conceptual Framework. Remember that the review of the theory has been done as a way of structuring the review of the empirical literature. You should, therefore, make the connection explicit. Suppose, for example, that a student researcher who proposes to study how student behavior affects teacher performance has developed the conceptual framework shown in Exhibit 10.5. The student might make the connection in this manner:

> As noted in the conceptual framework, a teacher's performance in any given class is a result of several interacting factors. Of all those factors influencing the teacher, the behavior of the students has perhaps received the least attention by researchers. Since student behavior is the focus of the proposed research, the review of the empirical literature that follows will review all the published studies on the interaction of student behavior and teacher performance.

Organize the Review of the Empirical Research. Your review will be more effective if it has a clear organization. Simply listing the studies is not sufficient. You have to organize the studies in some coherent manner and make that pattern clear to your reader. In general, you can organize the review in one of the following ways:

1. Chronological. Use a time pattern if there have been trends or developments in the knowledge base over time. For example, a review of the literature on outcomes-based education might use a chronological order, since there were definite trends in its use over a 20-year period.

2. Opposing camps. If you are reviewing an issue about which researchers have reached different conclusions, then it might be helpful to organize them accordingly. If, for example, you propose to study the

grouping of academically gifted students, you might organize the review in this manner:

Studies supporting homogeneous grouping

Studies supporting heterogeneous grouping

3. Conceptual. Perhaps the most common pattern of research reviews involves a conceptual analysis in which you identify the major concepts or factors appearing in the literature. For example, the research on teachers' professional development might be organized in this manner:

Studies of teachers' cognitive development

Studies of teachers' moral development

Studies of teachers' career development

Be sure to make clear to the reader which organizational pattern you are using.

Review the Research. You then use that organizational pattern to review the research. The review in the comprehensive proposal should be fully developed, with studies described sufficiently for the reader to understand their findings. In the working proposal, you could use either of two summary forms. Exhibit 10.6 shows a form that emphasizes the researcher; Exhibit 10.7, one that emphasizes the findings.

Relate the Review to Your Study. Finally, be sure to relate the review of the research to your own study. Make clear to the reader the connection between what has been learned in the past and what you propose to do. Here is how one student researcher made that connection:

As the above review indicates, teachers tend to have negative feelings about curriculum monitoring systems.

Exhibit 10.6 Summary Form Emphasizing
Researcher

Mentor Problems		
Researchers	*Date*	*Finding*
Feiman-Nemser & Floden	1986	Expert status of mentors questioned in the culture of teaching
Smylie & Denny	1989	Expert status not accepted by rest of teachers

Exhibit 10.7 Research Summary Emphasizing
Findings

Mentor Problems

1. Mentors are given an expert status. However, in the culture of teaching, such status is suspect, since teachers tend to have an egalitarian perspective. (Feiman-Nemser & Floden, 1986; Smylie & Denny, 1989)

This proposed study will examine whether those negative feelings are found when teachers are held accountable for student achievement on end-of-course tests.

DEVELOPING THE PROPOSAL: WRITING CHAPTER 3

Chapter 3 includes a detailed explanation of the proposed methodology. Note that both the full and the working proposal present the methodology in detail. Along with the problem statement, the explanation of the methodology is the most important part of the proposal.

Presenting the methodology in full detail accomplishes two goals: It enables you to systematize your decisions about the methods you plan to use, and it enables your committee to ensure that the methodology is sound.

Be sure to organize the discussion of the methodology in a logical manner. Although the specific organization will vary with the type of research, in general this pattern will apply for most studies.

1. Type of research and specific subtype

2. Context and access

3. Participants and how selected

4. Instrumentation

5. Data collection

6. Data analysis

Review Chapter 9 for a discussion of the specific issues to be examined in the methodology section.

DEVELOPING THE PROPOSAL: THE REFERENCES

The reference section should include all references used within the document. The reference section should follow the appropriate reference style required by your institution.

DEVELOPING THE PROPOSAL: THE APPENDICES

The appendix will include any supporting materials, such as copies of instruments. It should also include a copy of your planning schedule or a summary of it.

HOLDING THE PROPOSAL DEFENSE

The proposal defense should be a relatively simple matter if you have followed the procedures explained in previous chapters. The assumptions are that you have held and profited from a preproposal conference and/or a miniproposal and have done the additional work required.

Coordinate Committee Schedules: Date and Time

It is important to seek advice from your committee chair on dates and times to consider when scheduling a proposal defense. Your committee chair may hold historical information regarding best dates and time frames, based on your committee membership, to conduct your proposal defense. It is a good practice to send an e-mail notice to committee members that includes several times and dates to conduct the proposal defense. Simultaneously, it is important to have discussed the facility location of the defense proposal with the respective department secretary, so include the secretary in those dates and times so that you will know what facilities are available. If you do not receive a common date and time for all committee members to attend, then send another e-mail with additional dates and times. Continue to repeat this process until you are able to secure a common date and time for all committee members to attend (keep in mind the committee members need a minimum of two weeks to read the proposal). Once you are able to confirm the date and time with your committee, immediately forward that information to the department secretary so that he or she may reserve the facility.

Prepare for the Proposal Defense

The defense will go well if you make certain preparations. First, prepare a good draft of your proposal. Ask the chair to review it before you submit it to the other members. Make any revisions suggested by the chair. Then confer with the chair to review the structure of the proposal defense and to identify other issues. The Proposal Conference Agenda form shown in Exhibit 10.8 should help you prepare for and participate in the proposal conference. The issues noted in the form are discussed in the following sections.

Presentation of the Proposal Defense

The structure of the defense will depend on the norms of your institution and the preferences of your committee. The form will help you and the chair clarify the major structural elements. Ordinarily, the dissertation chair will lead the proposal defense and will also note for the record any decisions or recommendations made. However, the chair may wish you to take a leadership role and to make your own notes. Most proposal conferences will last one hour; some may require additional time if major problems occur or if differences arise among the committee members.

Ordinarily, you should take from 15 to 30 minutes to present your proposal. A working proposal will probably take less time than a comprehensive proposal. Taking less than 15 minutes will seem too cursory; taking more than 30 minutes is simply unnecessary, assuming that your committee has read the proposal.

Facilities

Facilities vary at all institutions. Generally speaking, most institutions have several spaces equipped to conduct proposal defenses. This is a good question to ask your chair once you begin the dissertation process. Also, it is good practice to review the setup of the facility prior to your proposal defense so that the environment is familiar to you.

Exhibit 10.8 Proposal Conference Agenda

Student's name: _____ Date of conference: _____

Time and location of conference: _____

Research problem: _____

Dissertation committee: _____

_____

Preproposal conference: Has a preproposal conference
been held? If so, summarize its outcomes. _____

_____

Conference Structure

   1. Who will lead the session?_____

   2. Who will be responsible for making notes of decisions
      made?_____

   3. How long will the session probably last?_____

   4. About how much time should the student take to
      present the proposal? _____

Other Conference Issues

   1. Does the suggested time line for completion seem
      reasonable?

   2. What procedures should be followed in circulating
      chapters for committee review?

   3. What style manual should be followed in writing the
      dissertation? In the dissertation, how should the
      student-researcher refer to himself or herself?

   4. How should the dissertation be organized?

   5. What should be the scope of the literature review?

Location. The location of the defense is important to the
ease of the proposal defense process. The closer it is to
your committee's work location, the easier it is for your

committee to make arrangements to attend the proposal. Also, consider locations that are conducive for
other faculty (not on your committee) to attend.

Equipment. The equipment needed for the proposal
defense is a laptop computer and an LCD projector.
Again, checking the setup of the room and facilities can
answer such questions as the following: (1) Do I need to
bring an extension cord? (2) Does the facility have a laptop computer and LCD projector? (3) Do I need to be
shown how to operate the equipment?

Deal With Other Defense Issues

After the proposal itself has been reviewed, you
should ask the chair to discuss with the committee the
issues noted in Exhibit 10.8 if the issues have not previously been resolved. The committee should let you know
if the time line for completion seems reasonable from
their perspective. Will they be available for reviewing
chapters and meeting with you?

The issue of how chapters should be circulated is a
critical one. The following procedure is efficient both in
saving everyone's time and in maximizing committee
feedback:

1. You send Chapter 1 to your chair.

2. He or she reviews it and suggests revisions.

3. You revise and submit the revision to the chair, who
   reviews it and approves it (unless additional
   changes are needed).

4. You then use the same procedures with Chapters 2
   and 3, in succession.

5. When the chair has approved the first three chapters, he or she notifies the other committee members that those chapters are ready for their review.

6. You send the other committee members the approved drafts of Chapters 1, 2, and 3.

7. The other committee members send their suggestions for revision to the chair, who reviews them and confers with you about additional changes required for Chapters 1 through 3.

8. You revise Chapters 1 through 3.

9. You write Chapter 4 and send it to the chair, who suggests revisions.

10. You revise Chapter 4 and send the revised chapter to your chair.

11. You write Chapter 5 and send it to the chair, who suggests revisions.

12. You revise Chapter 5.

13. Your chair notifies the committee that all chapters have been approved and that you are ready for the dissertation draft.

14. You send the complete dissertation to the committee.

15. You make any final changes the other committee members request.

That set of procedures should simplify the complex process of working with your committee. Be sure to resolve this issue with the committee; do not assume that they will agree to use the procedures described above.

The proposal defense is also a good time to resolve the issue of writing style. Most education professors prefer that student researchers use the current edition of the *Publication Manual of the American Psychological Association.* One specific issue of writing style is how you should refer to yourself. The traditional style is to minimize the person of the researcher by using the passive voice of the verb or by using the term *the researcher,* as in these examples: "The tests were administered," "The researcher then interviewed the principal." However, many scholars now believe that a more direct style is preferable: "I then administered the tests," "I interviewed the principal."

You should also clarify the issue of dissertation organization. Here is the standard organizational pattern used in most quantitative studies:

1. Introduction to the study

2. Review of the literature

3. Methodology

4. Results of the study

5. Summary and discussion

However, this standard pattern does not work for many qualitative studies. For example, a case study of a math department might be organized in the following manner:

1. Introduction to the study

2. Selecting the site and gaining access

3. Phase 1: Making contact

4. Phase 2: Getting to serious work

5. Phase 3: Winding things up

6. Summary and discussion

The other key issue that you should resolve at the defense, if you have not done so previously, is the scope of the literature review. Does the committee prefer a broad review of all related issues or an in-depth, narrowly focused review? Also determine if the literature review should include an explanation of the search process you used and a review of the theoretical literature.

POSTPROPOSAL STEPS

Immediately following the proposal defense, it is important to meet with your dissertation chair to discuss next steps to continue progressing successfully in the dissertation process. Shortly after the proposal defense, schedule one to two hours with the committee chairperson to debrief on what edits, if any, are needed and to outline the next steps.

Secure IRB Approval

Once your dissertation committee has approved your dissertation proposal, a very important next step is to secure Institutional Review Board (IRB) approval to collect and analyze the data associated with your study. The IRB approval process was discussed in great length in Chapter 2, so refer to that specific part of the chapter for the IRB process. Generally speaking, most university IRB offices will send you an e-mail notification of the study approval and follow up with a hard copy of the official approval notification so that you may include that document in your dissertation.

IRB Certification: Student

IRB certification for you is required to conduct research at institutions that require IRB approval. Each IRB certification period is for a length of three years. The IRB organization will not notify you of when your certification will expire. It is your responsibility to ensure your certification is current. Therefore, it is important to be mindful of how and when this requirement is offered during your program of study.

IRB Certification: Adviser

IRB certification is also required of the dissertation director/adviser. It is important that you ask your chair if his or her IRB certification is current. As a side note, this becomes apparent when completing the IRB approval form. The form will require you to list your dissertation chair's certification date, and in some instances may require you to list the dissertation chair's IRB number.

University Requirements/Protocols

Following the defense proposal, each university has specific requirements for recognizing the approval of the proposal and how to proceed with the study. Universities often have proposal defense forms that must be signed and dated by all members of the dissertation committee noting the satisfactory, or unsatisfactory, proposal defense. For the purpose of this book and considering that you have followed very closely the suggestions outlined here, we will continue with the premise that the proposal defense was satisfactory. Once the dissertation committee has approved, the completion of the IRB request to conduct the study must be the very next activity that you engage in with you dissertation chair. Now, a suggestion: while you are awaiting IRB approval, this is an excellent time to make all revisions to Chapters 1 through 3 based on the feedback given from your committee during the proposal defense.

Collect Data After Obtaining Appropriate Approvals

Once you have obtained IRB approval, you may then begin collecting the data associated with your study. A caution: do not collect any data related to your study before you have received IRB approval. You must collect, store, and provide safeguards for the data just as you described in the IRB approval process. Any deviation from this without direct notification and approval from the IRB office is considered a violation of the research process and may cause your study to be revoked by the IRB office.

COMMITTEE REQUIREMENTS

The dissertation committee may require you to add, delete, and/or revise the content you presented during the proposal defense. Any of the aforementioned requests are natural occurrences within the dissertation process.

Required Edits and/or Revisions

The feedback you receive from the dissertation committee as a result of the proposal defense is beneficial to the success and improvement of your study. The committee may require you to make specific edits to the content and/or revise specific content for general flow and substance. Keep in mind that these edits/revisions are purposefully meant to focus the study so that you engage in quality research and the end result is a quality product that you and your respective university will be proud of.

Review and Adjust Time Line

Based on the amount of edits and revisions, you need to consult your chair to see if there may be a need to adjust your time line for your study completion. This adjustment really depends on the amount of work needed to make the necessary revisions and the time you have to commit to making the revisions. Once you and your dissertation chair have made a determination on your time line, it is time to continue working on your study by committing the resources to produce a quality study.

TECHNOLOGY TECHNIQUE: PAGE NUMBERING USING WORD PROCESSING SOFTWARE AND UNIVERSITY GUIDELINES

At the conclusion of the study, pagination is required and is about the final touch needed to complete the study. To complete the pagination, refer to the guidelines required by your specific university. Each university may have slightly different requirements for how pages are placed on the document. For example, some universities require a "bottom middle" page number; others require a "top right" page number. Regardless of requirement, it is imperative that you follow your university guidelines regarding pagination.

A technology technique that may be used as a consistent measure is the function included in your computer's software. Use the pagination function to format your document to meet the university requirements. A simple selection of the required style within your software and a click of the function button will apply the pagination on the entire document. Review the document to ensure charts and tables have been paginated properly.

Researching and Writing the Thesis or Dissertation

ELEVEN

Implementing the Research Design

With the proposal defense concluded and the necessary revisions to the proposal made, you are now ready to conduct the research according to research design. This chapter suggests some steps to follow to avoid problems with this critical part of your study.

COMMUNICATE PERIODICALLY WITH THE CHAIR

A common complaint of dissertation chairs is the student's failure to communicate. In too many instances, the student completes the proposal defense, encounters family and career problems that cause delays, and does not communicate with the chair for several months. The recommendation here is to send the chair a brief report every two weeks, even if there is nothing of significance to report. Most committee members will not require frequent communication; they assume that the chair is monitoring the student's progress. To simplify communication, you may wish to use your own version of the form shown in Exhibit 11.1.

Exhibit 11.1 Research Progress Report

Student: Ellen Stroud Chair: Dr. Justin L. Shore			
Research Step	Date Proposed	Date Accomplished	Comments
Contact participants	5/5	5/18	Death in researcher's family; teachers expressed concern about privacy

It is especially important to communicate with both the chair and the other committee members if you consider major changes in the problem statement or the methodology. You should detail the proposed changes in a memo to the committee, requesting their written approval. Remember that the document approved at the prospectus defense is a contract between you and the committee. Thus, any modifications need the entire committee's approval.

Ensure Access to the Research Site

Before beginning data collection, verify your ability to gain access to the research site. In some cases, district administrators or school boards change their minds about permitting the study. Usually, they worry about possible parent opposition—or the intrusiveness of the study. To minimize such occurrences, ask the district administrators or school system's superintendent to sign a written statement granting approval before you begin data collection. They are less likely to change their minds once they have agreed in writing to grant access. If they do deny access after initial approval, appeal the decision while making plans to find another site.

Avoid Premature Data Collection

Some students make a serious error by beginning the data collection before the proposal defense has been held. Although their desire to get a quick start on the research is understandable, this premature beginning is fraught with risks. The student's committee will be unhappy that its function has been short-circuited. Lacking final committee review, the instruments may be flawed. Proper access may not have been secured. In the unlikely event that the committee approves data collection before the proposal defense has been held, secure a written statement to this effect from the chair, and retain a copy in case you are questioned. If you have collected a substantial body of information without committee approval, apologize for your impulsiveness. Also, request assistance from the committee by reviewing the data that have been collected and by seeking assistance and guidance to bring the data into line with the research problem posed.

Develop a Detailed Planning Calendar

As suggested in Chapter 6, you should have developed a general planning calendar. Now it is time to develop a more detailed calendar for implementing the research. Exhibit 11.2 shows a calendar one student developed for a correlational study that examined the relationship between parents' technology familiarity levels and students' academic use of technology.

In developing the calendar, develop realistic deadlines that you are sure you can meet. Ask your chair to review your detailed calendar, and then try to adhere to the deadlines you have set.

Exhibit 11.2 Research Planning Calendar

Step	Date
1. Confirm access.	10/1
2. Secure copies of instruments.	10/15
3. Prepare orientation materials.	9/1
4. Orient teachers.	10/20
5. Orient students.	10/27
6. Administer student instruments.	11/1, 11/2
7. Administer teacher instruments.	11/1, 11/2
8. Compute and standardize student scores.	11/15–30
9. Compute and standardize scores.	12/1–15
10. Use statistical packages to compute correlations.	12/16–20
11. Review all data for accuracy.	1/2–15

CHANGE THE SCHEDULE AS NEEDED

You should be ready to change the schedule as the need arises, especially when unforeseen circumstances occur at the research site which required schedule alterations. Most doctoral studies in education involve schools and their faculties. As an educator, you know how unpredictable life can be in such situations. The most common result is a change in the school's schedule. Perhaps you had planned on a faculty meeting to be held in November as a time to orient the teachers; then the principal cancels the meeting or decides there is no time for your orientation. Plan a research schedule that is flexible and allows for modification. Reschedule your work as needed. When doing so, be sure that you do not alienate the administrators or teachers; your study is not the most important aspect of their professional lives.

PREVENT PROBLEMS WITH THE INTERVENTION

Many researchers have discovered to their dismay that the teachers did not implement the intervention as planned. Teachers tend to be independent when it comes to their classes, and many believe that they can do a better job than the researcher in implementing an intervention. You can take several steps to avoid problems of this sort.

Throughout the research, you should emphasize to the teachers that you see them as highly skilled professionals who are making a professional contribution by collaborating with you as equals. Whenever possible, you should involve the teachers in the planning process so that they feel some ownership of what is done. Also, you should provide them with the training needed to implement the intervention as required. When consistency in implementation is crucial to the research, some researchers have even developed written scripts for the teachers to follow.

USE COMPUTERS MINDFULLY

Most graduate researchers use the available software to aid in the data analysis process. Several packages are available for both quantitative and qualitative analyses; check with your committee about the best package currently available. You should use the software mindfully, however; that is, you should understand the processes at work. Understanding the processes will facilitate your interpretation of the results and will also enable you to respond thoughtfully at the defense if an issue of data analysis arises. Here are two examples to illustrate what is meant:

MINDLESS USE OF SOFTWARE PACKAGE: I used SPSS to do a t test. It wasn't significant. (Committee member asks, "What is the t test?") The t test is a test of significance.

MINDFUL USE OF SOFTWARE PACKAGE: I used SPSS to compute the *t* test. (Committee member asks, "What is the *t* test?") The *t* test is used to see if the observed difference between the mean scores of two groups on a measure is likely to have occurred by chance or if it represents a true difference in the scores of the populations.

Ensure a High Rate of Return on Surveys

Many student researchers develop survey studies and then, to their dismay, secure only a low rate of return. Cochran (1977) showed that nonresponse rates even as low as 20 percent may be sufficient to raise questions about the generalizability of the results. Although most experts in the field believe that researchers should aim for a 60 percent return, Kaplowitz, Hadlock, and Levine (2004) purport that some surveys with response rates lower than 50 percent are valid because there are no differences between responders and nonresponders, whereas some surveys with a 90 percent rate are biased.

You can prevent the problem of nonresponse by using an instrument that is very clearly written and easy to complete. You are also more likely to get a satisfactory return rate if you can convince the participants that your study is important and assure them that you will share the results with them. You can also ensure a high rate of return by having participants complete the survey instrument while they are part of an intact group, such as a faculty meeting.

If the initial rate of return is low, you should "follow up" with tactful reminders. If nonresponse rates are lower than 90 percent even after two reminders, Kaplowitz et al. (2004) recommend that you perform a *nonrespondent bias check* to determine if the nonrespondents are significantly different from the respondents on key variables.

Maintain Careful and Duplicate Records

Throughout the study, you should keep your researcher's journal and a search record. In addition, you should be sure to back up files and copy data. Although losing data is not a common occurrence, the problem occurs frequently enough to stress the importance of copies and backup files.

Technology Technique: Electronic Data Collection and Analysis

With today's technology, it is easy to generate an online or electronic survey, send an e-mail to the appropriate participants, and allow the survey host to collect the data. An Internet search engine such as Google can be used to obtain the names of multiple online survey tools, e.g., Key Survey (http://www.keysurvey.com); Survey System (http://www.surveysystem.com/online-surveys); Check Box (http://www.checkbox.com); Survey Monkey (http://www.surveymonkey.com); and so on. Most online survey hosts allow a survey to be created and uploaded to a web page for use in collecting data. Some may provide descriptive statistics. Yet it is the researcher's responsibility to secure and/or prepare a valid and reliable data collection instrument. By using online survey tools, the time to collect data is reduced, but the integrity of the collected data depends on the quality of the data collection instrument. Regardless of the online survey tool used, researchers must follow the same guidelines or procedures as if they were using a hard copy, or paper, survey. The technology is only a tool, and the credibility and believability of the results are only as good as the quality of the data collection instrument and process.

Mastering the Academic Style

Before examining the issue of how to write specific chapters of the dissertation, it might be useful at this juncture to closely examine the goal of mastering academic style. The academic style is a style of writing that is expected in term papers, theses, dissertations, and scholarly articles. Notice that this book is not written in an academic style, since it is intended as a technical manual of advice written for graduate students.

FOLLOW THE RECOMMENDED STYLE GUIDE

At the outset, be sure you have available and refer to the approved style guide adopted by the institution that will grant the degree. Check with your chair to see which is recommended. If you have a choice, use the most recent edition of the *Publication Manual of the American Psychological Association*. Also observe the guidelines specified by ProQuest, UMI Dissertation Publishing, or the appropriate dissertation/thesis repository used by the institution granting the degree. Furthermore, if the university conferring the degree requires electronic submission of dissertations, then by all means secure and follow those guidelines and requirements. Institutional guidelines may supersede the institution's adopted style manual.

1. Use high-quality white paper, minimum 20-pound weight, 8½ by 11 inches. Do not use erasable paper.

2. Double-space all text. Long quotations and footnotes may be single-spaced.

3. Use a 10-point or 12-point font.

4. Use a laser printer.

Most style manuals also recommend that you use a left margin of 1½ inches, to provide room for binding.

USE THE WRITING PROCESS

Mastering a basic process for writing should help at all stages of the dissertation. What you learn about using a good writing process for the dissertation should be of help in future academic writing tasks.

What writing process should you use in writing the dissertation? The answer is a complex one, since individuals vary so much. There is not too much guidance from the research. There are several studies of how professional writers write novels and hundreds of studies of how students write essays but few studies on how graduate students write theses and dissertations. The standard process model taught to secondary students (prewrite, draft, edit, revise, publish) is not useful when it comes to writing dissertations. However, by reviewing the available research and by reflecting on personal experience, it is possible to offer some general guidelines that should keep you in good stead.

Develop an Effective Approach to Writing

Before looking at the specific tasks of writing one chapter, it might be useful to consider some general guidelines for developing an effective approach to writing.

First, ensure that you have ready access to a computer and good word processing software. The computer is a scholarly necessity: It greatly facilitates the writing process; it makes revision a relatively simple matter; it provides access to databases; and it simplifies the data analysis task. Thus, the computer significantly reduces the time spent in completing the dissertation. Then, when you have finished writing the dissertation, it can continue to be of immeasurable help in your professional career, thereby eliminating the dependence on others for assistance in completing the dissertation.

Next, create a research/writing center for yourself. Your research and writing will be easier and faster if you obtain and maintain at the university or at home a special spot of your own where you do all your dissertation thinking and writing. Equip it with your research and writing needs: computer, files, dictionary, and related professional works. Reserve the center for dissertation work only so that every time you sit down in that special chair, the environment says, "dissertation thinking and writing time."

Also, develop a writing schedule that will help you write systematically and effectively. Since the general issue of developing and following a schedule was discussed in an earlier chapter of this book, it is probably sufficient to note here the need to schedule longer blocks of uninterrupted time on a regular basis—and to keep that time unaltered for dissertation writing. Most writers find that they need at least a three-hour block of time to be productive—to get some good writing done. You begin with a slow "warm-up" period, and then you hit your stride to find the writing flow. If you must stop when you feel your writing is going well, then you lose the momentum. Your writing time should, of course, be free of distractions; you can't write while you're watching the baby, doing the laundry, or watching television.

Finally, arrange for the help you will need. You may need to hire a professional word processor, if you do not do your own. If you do hire someone, make clear that you are contracting for word processing services, not "typing." You want your dissertation on flash or jump drives or CDs to simplify all the revising that will be needed.

You will also need an editor. An editor's function is to read very carefully your good drafts and suggest or make specific improvements in organization and style. The editor does not write for you; that is dishonest and unethical. But the editor does more than insert commas and correct your spelling; a good editor will suggest how the chapter might be reorganized, will note paragraphs that need fuller development, and will indicate how sentences can be rewritten. Every writer needs a good editor—and making use of a good editor will simplify the whole process for you. You should, of course, acknowledge the editor's help in the appropriate place in your dissertation.

This matter of using editing assistance is so delicate, however, that you should discuss it with your chair. Some universities provide specific policy guidelines to help students distinguish between the ethical practice of using an editor and the unethical one of using a ghostwriter. Some chairs may prefer that you not use an editor. In general, however, professors do not want to edit your writing. They are scholars, not editors.

Write With an Efficient Process

With that basic approach well established, you are ready to write one chapter. What is the best process to use here? As noted above, there is no single right answer. You have to experiment to find the process that works best for you. In general, however, you should find the following process a useful one.

Begin by systematizing your knowledge. The first step is to review and systematize what you know about the contents of that chapter. You think about what you have learned. You review your notes on the reading you have done. You reexamine your results. In this stage of systematizing your knowledge, you may find it helpful to talk into a tape recorder, think aloud, or discuss with a colleague. Or you may simply read and reflect. The important thing is to call to mind what you know and to start to think about a systematic way of ordering that knowledge.

Next, plan your chapter. With your knowledge reviewed and tentatively organized, you now should plan the chapter. How do you plan? You can simply adopt one of the outlines suggested in later sections of this work, since dissertation chapters tend to follow certain basic organizing patterns. You can read other dissertations like your own and follow a pattern that someone else has used. (Do not worry about the ethics of following someone else's plan; professional writers do it all the time.) Or you can start from scratch—beginning with nothing—and develop your own plan. If you start from scratch, there are two basic ways of developing a plan. Some writers plan from the "bottom up": They review their notes, put the notes in similar piles, identify the general topic of each pile, and then find a logical order for the general topics. Other writers plan from the "top down": They think about the contents of that chapter in an analytical fashion, determine the broad topics that need to be treated, and decide on a logical arrangement.

Regardless of the method you use, it probably is a good idea to reduce your plan to a written topical outline. You should ask your chair to review the outline before you begin writing that chapter; if the chair prefers not to review outlines, request assistance from a colleague whom you respect. The important rule to remember is that you should not begin writing a chapter until someone else has reviewed your outline. You may be convinced that your outline is excellent, but you are too close to your material to be a reliable judge of that matter. You need the input of an individual who is objective. Unless your chair requires a particular outline form, you should use any outlining system that is clear to you and others who will read it.

Then begin to write. Check your outline. Review your notes for the first section, and then start to write that section without worrying too much about style. What do you do if you have "writer's block"—that frustrating feeling that all writers know at times, when the words just will not come? The best answer is to write your way through it. Grit your teeth and write whatever comes into your head. Force yourself to write, even if the writing seems bad. Do not sit there and worry that you cannot write. If you do not know how to start the chapter, skip the introduction and jump right into the first major idea.

As you write, use headings and verbal signals to make your organization clear to the reader. The appropriate use of headings will help the reader track your organizational pattern. To understand this point, consider Exhibits 12.1 and 12.2. Exhibit 12.1 shows part of an outline of Chapter 2 of a study of techniques for questioning students; Exhibit 12.2 illustrates how the headings are used to clarify the organization. You should also use verbal signals that show where the chapter is going, such as *first, next, also,* and *finally.*

You should also revise as you write. Most good writers revise as they write, following a procedure that goes something like this:

Write a paragraph

Stop and read what was just written

Revise that paragraph

Write another paragraph and start the cycle all over again

How much revising you do and what you revise as you write are individual matters. Some writers are perfectionists. Especially if they are working on a word processor, they will

Exhibit 12.1   Partial Outline of Review of Literature:
Techniques for Questioning Students

I. Techniques for Questioning Students
   A. On task
      1. Clarification
      2. Solution checking
      3. Extension

   B. Requests

   C. Diversions

II. Frequency
   A. By subject

   B. By grade level
      1. Elementary
      2. Middle
      3. High

correct punctuation, tinker with sentences, and fret with word choice. Others do a quick draft without any revising and then polish the entire draft.

With that first draft finished, the best advice is to put it aside for a few hours at least and then read it with a fresh eye. Pretend you are the reader, not the writer. See if the organization is clear, if the generalizations are well supported, if the sentences flow clearly and smoothly, and if the words sound right. And then revise to improve.

In the revising process, use the editing processes available with your word processing software. All will do a spell check. Remember that spell-check programs will not detect an error such as using *affect* when you should have used *effect.* Most programs will also provide a thesaurus, if you wish to avoid repeating a word and cannot think of an alternative. You can also use a style checker, such as *WhiteSmoke*, which will suggest revisions based on the kind of style you have indicated.

Exhibit 12.2 Headings Corresponding to Outline

---

2. Review of the Literature

This chapter reviews the literature on techniques for questioning students, as a means of providing an intellectual background for the present study. The chapter organizes the review by examining the studies relating to four aspects of techniques for questioning students: types of student questions, frequency of questions, teacher strategies to elicit questions, and effects of student questions.

Types of Student Questions

Researchers have categorized student questions in terms of three purposes: to accomplish the task, to make a request, and to divert the teacher from the task.

Accomplishing the Task

Students ask questions to enable them to accomplish the assigned task. Task-oriented questions tend to be of three types.

Questions of clarification. Most of the task-related questions involve questions of clarification. Reeves (1987) found that elementary students asked such questions more often than secondary students . . .

Send the revised chapter to your editor before forwarding it to your chair. Discuss any substantive changes with your editor, and then revise in accordance with the editor's suggestions and your own sense of what you want to do.

Now you can send the revised chapter to your chair, along with an outline. At this point, you will need to follow your chair's recommendations about the submission of chapters. Some chairs prefer to get one chapter in good shape before letting the other committee members see it; others prefer to get committee input at the draft stage. Even if your chair does not require an outline, it probably is a good idea to include one anyway. The outline shows that you have planned systematically and helps your chair read and respond.

Most students have found it helpful to include with their revised chapter a copy of the chair's or committee's previous suggestions for revision. A conversation should have already been held with the chair to clarify what documents, if any, should accompany a chapter being sent for the chair's review. Some chairs may want any previous drafts that contain revisions to be made to be included with the current chapter. Other chairs may want only the chapter. To be certain, communicate with your chair. By talking with your chair, you should minimize the problem of receiving conflicting messages with each subsequent revision.

MASTERING THE ACADEMIC STYLE

Academic writing is a unique genre that has its own norms. One of the implicit expectations of doctoral programs is that you will learn to write like a scholar. This section of the chapter offers some general advice about the sense of self you wish to project and then will deal with more specific applications.

Project an Appropriate Persona

Any discussion of the scholarly style should probably begin with an analysis of the scholarly persona. The persona is the public person you present in the writing—the image created by the writing. It results from several factors: the things you elect to discuss, the tone you adopt, the sentences you write, and the words you use. As a writer of a dissertation, you want to project the persona of a scholar; your writing should convey a message something like the following: "The writer is an informed and knowledgeable person who knows the norms and conventions of the profession, who has done some interesting and useful research, but who has the good sense to be suitably modest about it."

Below are listed some general suggestions for achieving such an effect.

1. Strive for clarity. Many writers of dissertations struggle to sound scholarly and in the process of trying to achieve that effect, become confusing. The best scholarly writing is lucid, even to someone who is not an expert in the field. Clarity is essentially a matter of ordering your sentences so that the parts clearly relate to each other and choosing your words so that they are readily understood. Clarity also comes about when you arrange the parts in a systematic way and make that arrangement clear to the reader.

2. Project maturity. Your sentences should sound mature. The following discussion will explain how such an effect is achieved; the point is that your concern for clarity must be balanced with a concern for maturity. You could write in a very simple style that would be clear and easy to read, but it might sound "just a bit too immature" for the readers of your dissertation.

3. Project a sense of formality. As mentioned in an earlier chapter, the dissertation is expected to be more formal in its style than most of the writing that you do. While there is a clear tendency to move away from the stilted formality that characterized most academic writing a couple of decades ago, there is still the expectation that you will not sound informal or colloquial.

4. Strike an appropriate balance between confidence and tentativeness. Many dissertation writers fall into the trap of claiming too much. The problem they have studied is the most important one, the need is most urgent, and the study proves beyond a doubt that such a finding is true. The answer here is to use the

language of tentativeness: *it is likely that, it seems obvious here, one tentative conclusion that might be drawn* . . . On the other hand, don't overdo the tentativeness by qualifying every statement you make. Consider three examples to illustrate the point:

TOO CONFIDENT: The study proves that students who are taught by national board certified teachers perform higher on standardized tests than students who are NOT taught by national board certified teachers.

TOO TENTATIVE: One conclusion that might be drawn from this study is that at this particular school, on the basis of this investigation, that students taught by national board certified teachers seemed to earn higher scores on standardized tests than students who were *not* taught by national board certified teachers.

BETTER: The findings suggest that most students at this school who were taught by national board certified teachers had higher scores on standardized tests than students who were *not* taught by national board certified teachers.

Most important of all, document your assertions. This matter is so important that perhaps it needs special examination.

Document Assertions

One mark of the scholarly paper is that assertions are documented: The writer provides evidence for statements that might be reasonably challenged. In contrast, the paper written for a mass audience or one written by a novice typically abounds in generalizations without evidence. The journalist writes: "Experts now believe that most large employers will soon be providing child care services for working parents." The scholar writes:

> According to several studies, a large percentage of the companies employing more than 1,000 employees provide some form of child care for working parents. (See, for example, the Murphy, 1997, survey.)

In writing a dissertation, documentation is essential, since the dissertation is scholarly in nature. This means that you should provide evidence for every general statement that is open to challenge.

There are three general approaches to handling this problem. One way, obviously, is to avoid it: Couch the observation in a way that does not require documentation. Contrast these two versions:

1. Schools are more and more getting back to the basics.

2. A reading of both professional journals and the popular press during the past few years strongly suggests that many public school administrators and teachers are more concerned with what is loosely termed "the basics."

The first statement is open to challenge: Which schools? How many? Do you mean pupils, parents, teachers, or administrators? What evidence do you have? What basics? The statement requires either careful documentation or extensive revision. The second statement is more cautious and also more specific. It makes a general observation about how the popular and professional publications are concerned with the issue; it specifies "administrators and teachers" instead of the vague "schools"; it uses words like *suggests* and *many* to indicate tentativeness; and it admits that there is some vagueness about the term *the basics*. It is wordy, but it is a defensible assertion couched in a way that does not require documentation.

A second choice is to offer in the text itself the evidence that supports the assertion. This example illustrates this second choice:

There has been in recent years increased interest in cooperative learning among both researchers and practitioners. A survey of the entries in *Current Index to Journals in Education* for the years 1985 through 1995 indicates that . . .

Here you provide the evidence directly, noting the facts that support the general assertion. The third and more commonly used option is to cite other sources that provide the evidence. You refer the reader to the literature that provides the support for the claim you make. Here is an example of this approach:

Several years ago, researchers turned their attention to interactive and recursive models of the composing process (Applebee, 1987; Graves, 1985).

Now, in making citations to support assertions, you are expected to demonstrate scholarly integrity:

- Do not cite sources you have not read.
- Wherever possible, cite primary, not secondary, sources.
- Do not distort the source; don't twist the evidence just to support your own notions.

You can overdo this documentation, of course—*but when in doubt, document*.

Vary the Way You Identify Sources

There are several ways to cite sources. Suppose, for example, you wish to cite a 2004 study by Boldt that concluded that public school superintendents' certifications vary state by state. Here are several ways you can cite this source:

- According to Boldt (2004), certification require-
  ments for superintendents vary . . .
- Boldt (2004) concluded that . . .
- Certification requirements for superintendents vary
  state by state (Boldt, 2004).
- In the 2004 study by Boldt . . .

Vary the way you cite sources, to avoid excessive
repetition.

Use Appropriate Paragraphing

The length and structure of the paragraph play an
important part in the scholarly style. The length of a paragraph is primarily a factor of format and audience. Articles
printed in a journal with very narrow columns tend to be
divided into shorter paragraphs to increase readability;
paragraphs in textbooks tend to run longer, unless written
for an immature audience. Shorter paragraphs are easier
to read, or at least look easier to read; longer paragraphs
seem more difficult. Besides factors of format and audience, the most important concern is the way your ideas
and information are segmented. Textbooks on writing
usually advise that each paragraph should be about one
main idea. In general, that is good advice; all other things
being equal, divide a paragraph when you think you have
come to the end of an idea or set of information. A good
rule of thumb to keep in mind in writing dissertations is
this: write main paragraphs of about 100 to 150 words in
length or longer, or approximately eight to ten sentences.
Very short paragraphs, as noted above, might give the
impression of an immature style or shallow thinking; paragraphs that are too long do not invite the reader to read.
Also, be sensitive to the norms of your own profession,
since there seem to be differences here. Paragraphs in
science reports, for example, tend to be shorter than
those in education articles.

In terms of the structure of the paragraph, remember that paragraphs in scholarly writing tend to move from the general to the specific. You begin the paragraph with a general statement and then provide the specifics to develop and support that general statement. Occasionally the order is reversed: The paragraph begins with specifics and ends with a generalization. Ordinarily, however, the general-to-specific pattern is easier for the reader to follow and understand. In both situations, a concluding transitional sentence is an effective tool to connect the ideas from the previous paragraph to the forthcoming paragraph.

Write Clear, Mature Sentences

It is not feasible in this book to present a full treatment of sentence structure and sentence effectiveness; instead, this discussion can only highlight some general features of the scholarly sentence and offer some general points of advice. Readers interested in a more extensive treatment of the sentence should consult any handbook on writing style and usage; several excellent ones are available in university bookstores. This discussion concentrates on those issues that are most important in the dissertation.

1. Combine shorter sentences. Shorter sentences suggest immaturity. Consider these examples:

   TOO SHORT: Sawyer (2008) studied the effectiveness of the new schedule. Scores on the Stanford Achievement Test were used as the measure.

   COMBINED: Sawyer (2008) studied the effectiveness of the new schedule, using scores on the Stanford Achievement Test as the measure.

2. Put the main idea in the main clause. The main clause is the part of the sentence that can stand by itself; it should contain the main idea. The mistake of putting

the main idea in a subordinate structure is called "incorrect subordination." Here is an example:

INCORRECT: The schedule was in effect only one year, with students achieving better results.

BETTER: Students achieved better results, although the schedule was in effect only one year.

3. Reduce the number of *and*s. Excessive use of the conjunction *and* suggests a childish style. Consider these two examples:

TOO MANY ANDS: The teacher put the assignment on the board, and then she checked the roll and found that three students were absent.

BETTER: After putting the assignment on the board, the teacher checked the roll and found three students absent.

4. Achieve an effect of clarity and directness by expressing the main action of the sentence in the verb and the main doer of the action (the agent) in the subject. Scholarly writing especially suffers from the vagueness that comes from burying the action in a noun and using nonaction verbs like *do, make, have, be, perform,* and *occur.* Consider some examples:

VAGUE AND WORDY: Orientations and explanations are important methods used by teachers in teaching writing.

BETTER: Teachers teach writing by orienting and explaining.

Words such as *orientations* and *explanations* are called nominalizations. Nominalizations are nouns made from verbs: *orientation* from *orient, explanations* from *explain.* In general, avoid excessive nominalization.

5. Avoid inserting long modifiers between the subject and the verb. For the most part, a sentence is easier to read if the subject and verb are reasonably close. Consider these two examples:

TOO SEPARATED: School administrators who are interested in making changes that are not too expensive or too complex for the most part have been overly receptive to simplistic solutions.

BETTER: Since many school administrators seem interested in making only simple and inexpensive changes, they have been overly receptive to simplistic solutions.

6. Avoid using subordinate clauses that modify other subordinate clauses. This mistake is called "tandem subordination." It produces sentences like this one:

CONVOLUTED: One of the obstacles that deters the installation of solar energy systems that are designed to achieve the savings that are important to all people is the reluctance of those same individuals to make large capital investments.

BETTER: Many people are reluctant to install solar energy systems because of the large capital investment required.

7. Place modifiers so that they clearly modify what you intend them to modify. As your 10th-grade English teacher reminded you, participles and reduced clauses are especially troublesome in this regard. Be sure that every such modifier clearly relates to the appropriate antecedent. Here are two examples to illustrate this point:

INCORRECT: Having explained the directions, the students began to write.

CORRECT: After the teacher explained the directions, the students began to write.

8. Avoid excessive use of the passive voice. In the
passive voice, the receiver of the action is the subject and the doer is buried in a phrase, as in this
example:

PASSIVE: The test was taken by the students.

ACTIVE: The students took the test.

The third person with the passive was once considered desirable because it resulted in a detached, scholarly tone that hid the writer and seemed to connote
objectivity. It also resulted in a wordy, lifeless style illus-
trated by this sentence: "It was decided by this researcher
that the effects of socioeconomic status should be investigated as a factor that might possibly affect the amount
of reading done in the home."

This is more direct: "The researcher investigated the
relationship between socioeconomic status and the
amount of reading done at home."

9. Be consistent in matters of verb tense. This matter
gets complicated. Here are some general rules
that should work in most cases:

- Use future tense in the proposal: "A random sample of students will be selected . . ."
- Use past tense in the literature review, unless you
are referring to a current belief of the researcher,
as in these examples.

Slavin   (1990)   determined   that   individual
accountability . . .

Slavin (1996) indicates that his comprehensive
program . . .

- In the dissertation, use past tense for the design or procedure ("the sample was selected").
- In the dissertation, use present tense to describe and discuss the results that are there before the reader ("suggests that integrated programs . . .").

Some Special Matters of Word Choice and Form

For specific advice about word choice and usage, you should refer to one of the good usage reference works readily available. Also, of course, rely upon one of the standard style guides for matters of form. Check with your chair to determine which style guide is required. If none is specified, use the current edition of the *Publication Manual of the American Psychological Association.* It might be helpful, however, to note here a few specific matters that seem to cause special problems to writers of dissertations. A summary of these specific issues is presented in Exhibit 12.3.

Exhibit 12.3 Specific Matters of Style

Word Choice and Usage

1. Use jargon with discrimination. *Jargon* is the special language of your profession; it is so essential in discourse among professionals that you would have difficulty communicating clearly without it. Minimize your use of jargon and avoid terms that seem outdated or used too often.

2. Avoid fad expressions that have a brief vogue in your profession and then disappear. Most educators are tired of hearing about "paradigm shifts," for example.

3. Avoid colloquial expressions. Colloquial expressions (such as *a lot, write up, tracked down, checked up on*) are not appropriate in the dissertation.

4. Avoid the use of contractions, such as *it's, they're, didn't.* Their use is too colloquial.

5. Avoid adjectival nouns. English has a vital capacity for making adjectives out of nouns; consider, for example, such combinations as *steel door, school teacher, street sign*. Try to avoid such awkward combinations, however, as these: *achievement test, data analysis, school administration theory studies*, and *writer anxiety test results*.

6. Avoid the vague use of *we* and *our*. These pronouns are often ambiguous as to whom they refer. Here is an example of ambiguous use: "We should be more concerned with student responsibility." This is a clearer version: "Educators should be more concerned with student responsibility."

7. Avoid the second person *you* (and the imperative mode) unless you wish to communicate very directly with your readers. The imperative states a command or wish, without using the pronoun *you*: "Consider the next issue." Notice that this book makes extensive use of *you*—and the imperative mode—but this is not a research report.

8. Avoid the sexist use of the masculine pronoun in referring to males and females. Use the plural forms since they are not gender specific.

   SEXIST: A teacher should avoid imposing his opinions on students.

   BETTER: Teachers should avoid imposing their opinions on students.

9. The word *data* is usually considered plural. Write: "These data are . . ." Some dictionaries now note that the word is often used as a singular noun ("this data was . . .")—*but the plural is probably safer*.

Punctuation

10. The comma and the period always go inside the quotation mark. Here is an example of correct punctuation:

Although many researchers have analyzed organizations as "loosely coupled systems," only a few have bothered to define what is meant by "loose coupling."

(Continued)

(Continued)

Direct Quotation and Paraphrase

11. Use direct quotation only when it is important to preserve the exact words of the original. In most cases, paraphrase.

Format

12. Avoid the use of boldface and italics, if possible. Be certain to consult the style manuals and requirements for the university granting the degree. Use underlining where appropriate.

13. Use double spacing for the narrative. The *APA Publication Manual* recommends that you use single spacing for table titles and headings, figure captions, references (with double spacing between references), footnotes, and long quotations. That style manual also recommends using a triple space or two double spaces after chapter titles, between major subheadings, and before and after tables in the text.

Use of Tables

14. Use tables to present complex data. In the text itself, refer the reader to the table, commenting on the highlights without simply repeating what is included in the table.

TECHNOLOGY TECHNIQUE: TOOLS FOR WRITING SOFTWARE

Software exists for assisting with the writing process. Such software may be grouped into three categories: spell check, grammar check, and style check. Some of the software is provided with word processing programs, whereas other software may need to be purchased separately.

For example, word processing programs may include both a spell-check and a grammar-check component. Typically, the spell-check component verifies the spelling of words; but it does not check word usage. Furthermore, the

grammar-check programs included with word processing software are limited because they may suggest only a different sentence structure. However, grammar-check programs for purchase generally provide more substantial grammar support by checking word usage, punctuation, and so on. Examples of grammar-check software for purchase are these: Instant Grammar Checker (http://www.grammarly.com); Ginger Software (http://www.gingersoftware.com); Grammar Check Software (http://www.whitesmoke.com); and Grammar Software (http://www.grammarsoftware.com). Most grammar-check software vendors provide a free trial version.

For style-check software to work efficiently, the researcher must obtain and enter the bibliographic information in the appropriate field(s) within the software. If the citation is entered correctly, the style-check software is designed to generate both the appropriate "in-text" citation and also the bibliographic information for the reference list(s). Examples of such software are these: StyleWriter (http://www.stylewriter-usa.com); ScholarWord (http://www.scholarword.com); Citation (http://www.lib.calpoly.edu); and Purdue OWL (http://www.owl.english.purdue.edu). Style-check software is not without its problems. First, the successful generation of an in-text citation or a reference list depends on the information entered by the researcher. If the researcher fails to collect a vital piece of information for referencing a document such as an issue number, the software may not generate the reference. Second, if the data entered are correct, the software may not generate a reference list because of incompatibility with the word processing software used. Before electing to use such software, researchers should verify that the style check software is compatible with the word processing and spreadsheet software used.

Grammar-check and style-check software may be cost prohibitive for graduate students if the software must be purchased. Check with the institution granting the degree because it may have a site license for the software. If the institution has such a license, then it is available for your use either free or at a reduced cost.

Regardless, if you use spell-check, grammar-check, or style-check software, the drafts of the document must be read and proofread by a person. Although such software is a tool for verifying spelling, grammar, and style, a person must review to ensure that it is correct and nothing was overlooked. Remember, spell-check, grammar-check, and style-check software is only as good as the programmer, and a human mind is needed to complete the process. Graduate students can be assured that the software is as accurate as it can be; a person needs to review to verify that the software is correct. Your name will appear on Your document, and it is a reflection of you! You do not want any readers to find any errors.

THIRTEEN

Organizing the Dissertation

How are dissertations organized? What guidelines or principles govern the organization of individual chapters? How can the organization be made clear to the reader? And how is the dissertation finally packaged? These are all important issues that confront the doctoral student from the outset. This chapter examines these questions in the order posed.

HOW ARE DISSERTATIONS ORGANIZED?

The answer to this question is simple: in whatever way enables you to communicate your results clearly to the reader. Techniques of organization have no intrinsic value; they operate only to facilitate communication—to help you achieve your goal of informing the reader. Obviously, the particular organizational strategy you choose will be affected by such considerations as the nature of your study, the field in which you are working, the preferences of your dissertation chairperson, the particular requirements of your department, and the regulations imposed by the institution granting the degree.

There is a general pattern used in most dissertations. It is widely used, not just because it is sanctioned by tradition, but because it has its own internal logic. It is a pattern that provides answers to five fundamental questions:

1. What is the problem that I studied? This typically is the concern of the first chapter. The specific content of that first chapter is discussed more in detail below.

2. How does my study relate to previous work? This is the review of the literature, usually Chapter 2.

3. What methods did I use to study the problem? Chapter 3 typically is an explication of the methodology.

4. What results did I obtain? The reporting of the results might require more than one chapter.

5. What does it all mean? The dissertation ends with a summary and discussion of the results.

As noted, above, there are many variations to this basic pattern. In some cases, you might feel that a review of the literature would be better integrated into the rest of the dissertation rather than standing as a separate chapter unto itself. In some dissertations, the methodology is so implicit in the nature of the inquiry that you might feel that no separate treatment is needed. Some faculties now require the student to produce a publishable article instead of writing a standard dissertation. Thus, the graduate student has flexibility in organizing the final document; institutional guidelines must be followed regardless.

To illustrate more clearly this notion that the organization of the dissertation can vary with the nature of the study, consider the following plan for a qualitative dissertation.

Qualitative Study of Workplace Skills Needed for the 21st Century

Chapter 1. Introduction

Chapter 2. Methodology

Chapter 3. Phase 1: Workplace Skills Needed

Chapter 4. Phase 2: Workplace Skills Possessed

Chapter 5: Phase 3: Comparison and Contrast of Needed and Possessed Workplace Skills

Chapter 6: Summary and discussion with implications for educators

Rather than writing a separate chapter reviewing the literature, the student decided, with the approval of the chair, to integrate the literature review wherever appropriate.

If you feel at all *uncertain* about the best order, "stand back" from your study, consider your readers, develop a tentative plan for the order of chapters, and talk with your chair. It is very important to keep the lines of communication open at ALL times.

WHAT PRINCIPLES GOVERN THE ORGANIZATION OF INDIVIDUAL CHAPTERS?

First, each chapter must seem to relate to the whole. The reader should have the feeling that he or she is reading a unified narrative, not a collection of individual pieces. Next, each chapter should make sense by itself, organized in such a way that the reader can easily follow the line of argument. Finally, the parts of the chapter should clearly relate to each other, conveying a sense of order and form. Also, be sure to frame each chapter with a definite introduction that opens the chapter and suggests what is to come and a clear conclusion that draws the chapter to a close.

The organizational patterns found in most disserta-tions are summarized in Exhibit 13.1. The suggestions presented in Exhibit 13.1 are not intended as a rigid for-mula. They are offered only as typical patterns. If they seem useful to you with your dissertation, use them. Be certain that each chapter has its own sense of order.

HOW CAN THE ORGANIZATION BE MADE CLEAR TO THE READER?

This is an important issue, for if the organization is clear only to you, then you have failed in communicating with the reader. You have an obligation to make your plan clear, to provide the reader with a verbal road map so that the journey is made without detours. It is probably wiser to err on the side of overemphasizing the plan. Readers will forgive you more readily for providing too many maps than they will for confusing them.

You begin by indicating in Chapter 1 how the disserta-tion is organized. You open each chapter by linking it with the previous chapter and by indicating what will come. In this manner, you provide the reader with an overall framework for the dissertation.

Then you use headings and subheadings at the major divisions of the chapter. As each division begins, you use a transition paragraph or a transition sentence to illus-trate the connection between that division and what has been discussed previously. A transition paragraph is a short paragraph that links major sections of the paper. The first sentence leads the reader to consider the infor-mation presented in the previous section or division, and the second sentence directs the reader to the forthcom-ing discussion. A transition sentence has the same struc-ture in condensed form: The first part of the sentence, usually a subordinate clause, looks back. The second part, usually the main clause, looks ahead.

Exhibit 13.1 Typical Organizational Pattern

Chapter and Emphasis	Typical Pattern
1. Introduction and statement of the problem:	a. General background of the study b. Problem statement c. Professional significance of the problem d. Overview of the methodology e. Delimitations/limitations of the study f. Definitions of key terms g. Organization of the dissertation
2. A review of the literature:	a. An overview of how the chapter is organized b. Review of the theoretical and empirical literature, organized according to a particular pattern described by the author c. A summary of what the previous research seems to mean and how it relates to this study
3. The methodology of the study:	a. A description of the general methodology b. The research context or site c. The subjects or participants d. The instruments and materials used e. The procedures followed f. The data analyses made g. A summary statement of the methodology
4. The results of the study:	a. An overview of the chapter b. A presentation of the results, organized in terms of how the problem statement was posed in the first chapter c. A summary in general terms of the results obtained

(Continued)

(Continued)

5. The summary and discussion:	a. A summary of the results, organized in terms of how the problem statement was posed b. A discussion of the findings c. A rationale for each conclusion, implication, and recommendation

Here is an example from the dissertation on student academic performance. Assume that the writer has finished writing the section on types of instruments used for measuring student academic performance. Here is the transition that might be used to lead into the next section on the reliability and validity of such instruments: "In addition to this examination of the types of instruments, researchers have considered the reliability and validity of instruments used to measure academic performance." Notice that the first part of the sentence looks back, and the second part, ahead.

You also use paragraphing effectively as a tool to organize the document. You do not begin and end paragraphs whimsically, when the spirit moves you. You end a paragraph when you have fully developed an idea. You begin a new one when you are ready to move to a new idea. Keep in mind the caution noted in Chapter 12: Dissertations call for longer paragraphs. The longer paragraph suggests seriousness, formality, scholarship, and depth. Aim for a 100-word minimum—approximately six keyboarded lines. That seems arbitrary, of course. The point is that much shorter paragraphs—one or two sentences—will seem superficial.

Consider also the use of topic sentences as aids to organizational clarity. The topic sentence is a sentence that states the main idea of the paragraph. Topic sentences usually come first in expository prose, when they are used. Professional writers do not use or think about topic sentences. However, they are of help to the writer learning the craft. They give shape to the paragraph, and they help the reader. They say very clearly, "This is what this paragraph is about."

Here is an example of a topic sentence that ties the rest of the paragraph together:

> Basic requirements to teach in the various states across the nation vary. Every state requires teachers to be college graduates. However, states may require differing minimum scores on the national teaching exam known as the PRAXIS, which is required to be fully certified as a teacher. . . .

At the beginning of paragraphs and within a paragraph, make appropriate use of transition devices. A transition device is any expression or verbal strategy that helps the reader make connections. These are the devices most typically used:

1. Using a counting word: *first, second, next, finally.*

2. Using an expression that shows the relationship of ideas: *on the other hand, however, as a result, furthermore, consequently, moreover, yet, hence,* and so on.

3. Repeating a key word, as in this example: "Yet the philosophical view attempts to define profession in two ways—the 'Cartesian' and the 'Socratic.' The *Cartesian* approach to defining professions tries to make sense of a person's mind."

4. Using a pronoun that refers to a key term, as in this example: "Apparently, National Board Certified Teachers feel *they* are making a difference in the quality of education being provided to students."

Excessive use of such transition devices can seem heavy-handed. It may make more sense if you think about a basic matter of raising and meeting expectations.

Scholars who have studied coherence in English have stressed that coherence, the quality of seeming to stick together, really seems to emerge when the writer first raises certain expectations in the reader and then meets those expectations. Writing that seems disconnected either is not clear about the expectations or fails to meet the expectations raised.

Perhaps that basic notion summarizes all this advice about organization: Make clear to the reader what you plan to do—and then keep that bargain, clarifying how you have kept it.

How Is the Dissertation Finally Packaged?

The order and appearance of the final dissertation package are important matters: Check with your adviser about any special requirements of your university and consult whatever style manual is recommended. A standard order is presented below, with some brief comments where appropriate (see Chapter 19 for additional details).

Abstract. Remember that the abstract will probably appear by itself in one of the retrieval services—be sure it reads well, describes your study accurately, and seems self-contained. State the problem clearly, indicate briefly the methodology used, summarize the results, and comment briefly about their implications. Do not include any bibliographic references, tables, figures, abbreviations, or acronyms. Abstracts have a limited number of words, and the number of words allowed is mandated by the institution granting the degree.

Title page. In choosing a title, remember that it should be brief, descriptive, and clear. In thinking of a good title, ask yourself this question: "If I were another reader trying to find this study, what search terms would I use?" The answer should indicate to you what terms are important to include. Do not include phrases like *a study of, an investigation of.* Also keep in mind the scholarly impact of using a colon in your title: Many scholarly books, articles, and dissertations use a colon in the title. Here are two examples to illustrate these points.

POOR TITLE. The Effects of Video Display Terminals in Proofreading

BETTER TITLE. A Comparison of Errors Detected: Video Display Terminals Versus Hard Copy

Approval page. In some institutions, the approval of the committee and the dean of the college or school are indicated on the title page; in others a separate page is included. Be sure to follow the guidelines of the institution granting the degree.

Acknowledgments page. Most dissertations include an acknowledgment page in which the writer acknowledges the assistance received. It is expected that you will acknowledge the assistance of the committee, paying special tribute to the role the adviser played. You also should acknowledge any special financial support from funding agencies. You should note any editorial help you have received. And if you wish, you may acknowledge the assistance of a long-suffering spouse. But keep this section brief, and don't be too effusive.

Contents. Call the page Contents, not Table of Contents, unless university requirements specify Table of Contents.

List of tables and figures.

The chapters. Present them in the order that you think is clearest.

References. Most dissertations end with a list of references, with only works cited in the dissertation itself.

Appendices. Include in the appendix (or appendices) any supporting material that does not seem to belong in the main body of the dissertation.

Some universities expect an index to be included; follow your university's requirements if an index is required.

TECHNOLOGY TECHNIQUE: EDITORS/STYLE EDITORS

As mentioned previously, the student needs to ask other people to read, critique, and edit his or her written document. The individual who is asked to read the document should review for readability to determine if a reader can understand what has been written. In addition, an editor should suggest ways to improve the quality of the document. Only a person can verify that the document says something. In Chapter 12, style-check software was mentioned, but a style editor—a person—is needed. The style editor is an individual who is familiar with the documentation requirements of the institution granting the degree—this person is to verify the format of the bibliographic information both within the text and within the reference list. Technology is limited in what it can do; however, human ability and capability is needed to ensure that another person can locate your source if necessary.

FOURTEEN

Writing the Introductory Chapter

The first chapter seems to present special problems to writers of dissertations. Perhaps it is the realization that finally they have to begin. Perhaps it is the fear of making a false start. More likely it is the problem of simply not knowing how to start. What do you include in the first chapter—and in what order?

To a certain extent, of course, the answers to those questions are determined by the type of research and the nature of the dissertation. The best way to learn how to write the first chapter of your dissertation is to read other dissertations similar to yours. You should also discuss the matter with your chair.

However, there is one general pattern that seems to work for most dissertations. It goes like this:

- Introduction to the chapter
- The background of the study
- The problem statement
- The professional significance of the study
- An overview of the methodology

- Limitations and delimitations of the study
- Definitions of key terms

The next sections of the chapter examine each of those components.

INTRODUCTION TO THE CHAPTER

This opening section's main function is simply to get the reader into the chapter somewhat gradually rather than jumping directly into the first substantive division. It can be as brief as one paragraph; it can be as long as three or more pages. If you prefer a briefer introduction, then begin with a paragraph something like this:

> This dissertation is a report of an ethnographic study of the teaching of writing. The study was based primarily upon the direct observation of a fifth-grade teacher in an urban school district who used an "experience" approach to the teaching of language arts. This first chapter of the dissertation presents the background of the study, specifies the problem of the study, describes its significance, and presents an overview of the methodology used. The chapter concludes by noting the delimitations of the study and defining some special terms used.

A paragraph of this sort is very direct and to the point: It states the problem of the research and tells the reader what to expect in the rest of the chapter.

If you do not like such a direct beginning, then you start with a more discursive and reflective opening. You might note the special professional conditions at the time of your study, you might reflect a bit on the broad concern your study addresses, or you might refer to the societal conditions that made the problem seem important. Here's an example of a somewhat more discursive opening paragraph:

The quest for a better reading program is one of those beguiling challenges that continue to intrigue educators even in a time characterized by cynicism about educational innovation. Even after decades of unproductive experimentation, scholars and educational leaders still search for the optimal curricular and instructional approach that will solve once and for all "the reading problem." Teachers implement whatever new approach seems to promise amelioration, as long as that new approach is not too discrepant with present practice.

The writer would then continue to comment on the search for a better program and slowly lead into the problem of the study—how a classroom teacher implements a new reading program.

Note two matters of style here. First, in referring to your study in this and subsequent chapters, use past tense: write as if the study is all over, even though it might not be when you are writing the first chapter: "This study examined . . ." Second, the introduction to the chapter does not have its own heading. The first page of Chapter 1 looks like the one shown in Exhibit 14.1. (Throughout this work all headings are handled in the style recommended by the *Publication Manual of the American Psychological Association;* check your own style guide for variations.)

THE BACKGROUND OF THE STUDY

This section is intended to provide a context for your study. It answers this question: "What special factors were at work that might possibly have influenced the conceptualization and execution of the study?" Ordinarily the "background" section will take only two to five pages, again depending upon the nature of your study and your own approach to writing. In this section you might deal with such special background factors as the following:

- The societal background: Developments and changes in the society that made the problem seem important
- The intellectual background: Major intellectual and philosophical movements of the time that provided a special context for the study
- The professional background: Developments in your field that made the problem seem worth studying
- The research background: New methods that seemed worth using or new theories that seemed to need testing; gaps in existing knowledge

Ordinarily personal factors are considered irrelevant in the dissertation; the dissertation is a scholarly report, and readers typically are not interested in you as the researcher. Also, local factors are typically not identified. The fact that your school district needed a new teacher evaluation system is not worth mentioning in a dissertation that you hope will have a much broader impact.

Exhibit 14.1   Example of Part of the Introductory Chapter

1. Introduction to the Study

This dissertation is a report of an ethnographic study of the teaching of writing. The study was based primarily upon the direct observation of a fifth-grade teacher in an urban school district who . . .

Background of the Study

It might be useful at this juncture to describe briefly the professional developments occurring at the time that influenced the study. First, it was conducted at a time when the public in general and . . .

THE PROBLEM STATEMENT

The problem statement is a very brief section, perhaps only one-half page, in which you state the problem as clearly as possible. Though brief, it is a crucial section, since the way you state the problem will directly influence the way you present and summarize the results. The way the problem is stated will vary with the nature of the study. Review the problem statement forms explained previously.

THE PROFESSIONAL SIGNIFICANCE OF THE STUDY

With the problem stated, you turn next to the section concerned with the significance of the study. Your purpose here is simple: to answer the question, "Why did you bother to conduct the study?" In answering this question, your tone is important. You do not want to claim too much. Statements of this sort make readers bristle: "No other issue is more critical in the field of education today." You also need to be rather specific about the need or the significance, indicating by a careful analysis that the study is important from more than one point of view. Here are some of the ways in which you can argue for the study:

1. The general problem has intrinsic importance, affecting organizations or people.

2. Previous studies have turned up conflicting evidence concerning the specific issue that you have chosen to study.

3. Your study examines in a "real-life" setting the implementation of a program based on a theory that has been widely accepted but little tested.

4. The study is such that any meaningful results would seem to be of value to practitioners.

5. The population or the setting chosen is sufficiently unique that the study seems likely to advance knowledge in the field.

6. The methods you have chosen for the study have not been widely used in your profession, and your study will likely yield some useful methodological findings.

Notice that in each case you argue from a broad perspective; you do not claim significance by asserting that your organization benefited.

OVERVIEW OF METHODOLOGY

The next questions you should answer are "How did you conduct the study?" and "Which method did you use?" These questions will probably be answered fully in the chapter on methodology, but it seems useful to include in the first chapter a general statement of the method used to round out the introductory picture presented to the reader. Ordinarily a page or two of general discussion of methodology will be appropriate; be sure, of course, that you note that the issue is fully discussed at a later point in the dissertation. In your general discussion of methodology, you should note the research perspective, the research type, and the research methods in brief.

LIMITATIONS AND DELIMITATIONS

The limitations and delimitations of the study are important; they define for the reader the parameters within which you conducted the research. Inherently, it needs to be communicated what the study does not intend to accomplish or what the design will not allow.

Students often misunderstand the special research meaning of *delimitations;* it does not mean "flaws" or "weaknesses." Such an interpretation results in an apology for the study, which prejudices the reader against the study at the very outset. Instead, the term should be construed as having these other two related denotations: the boundaries of the study and ways in which the findings may lack generalizability. In considering this matter of delimitations, you would examine such concerns as the nature and size of the sample, the uniqueness of the setting, and the time period during which the study was conducted.

The limitations of the study are the parameters placed on the methodology. These limitations need to be noted and briefly discussed so the reader understands the potential impact of the application and interpretation of results of the study (see Kline, n.d.).

DEFINITION OF TERMS

Your introductory chapter probably should include your definitions of special terms used in the study. Do not feel obligated to define terms that are generally understood by those in your profession. You should, instead, ordinarily include definitions only when one or more of these conditions pertain:

- The term is relatively new in your profession and has not gained general currency.
- The term is often used ambiguously in the profession, and you wish to give it some preciseness.
- The term is a general one, and you wish to use it in a rather special way.

Definitions are expected to be written according to a somewhat standardized pattern. You first state the term. Then you identify the broad class to which the term belongs, using the same part of speech as the term itself. Then you specify the particular ways in which that term differs from others in its class. Here's an example:

Alternative school: a public (not private or independent) school whose program is considered to be substantially different from standard educational programs, which students choose to attend rather than attending the school to which they would ordinarily be assigned.

Observe that the general class is identified: "a public school." The term being identified is next distinguished parenthetically from other classes (not private or independent); then the two important distinguishing features are noted.

In considering this matter of definitions, you might wish to keep in mind a distinction between "system languages" (the special terms and meanings used in a given scholarly discipline) and "common language" (the words and meanings used in everyday discourse). This distinction means that you should not invent new words when the existing system language is adequate. Also, keep in mind that words that have a special system meaning should not be used to denote their common languages meaning. For example, the word *significant* should not be used to mean "important" in a dissertation that will also use the term in its system sense of "having statistical significance."

The first chapter should probably conclude with a paragraph that looks ahead to the rest of the dissertation, indicating to the readers what they may expect. Such a conclusion is not obligatory, but some general type of ending is expected by the reader. Write a few sentences that say to the reader, "This chapter is finished; prepare for the next one."

Keep in mind, finally, that these suggestions about the opening chapter describe a general pattern that seems to work. Check with your dissertation adviser or your department about any special requirements or formats.

TECHNOLOGY TECHNIQUE: WORD PROCESSING

The ability to create user-friendly documents may ease the frustration associated with the logistics of the study.

That is to say, the more skill you acquire regarding word processing, the less time you may need to commit to formatting the document. This will afford you more time to spend on the research and content of the study. As for word processing skills, the ability to understand and apply the functions appropriately when formatting the document will decrease the likelihood that there will be a formatting issue once the dissertation is reviewed by the dissertation chair or the respective graduate school.

FIFTEEN

Writing the Review of the Literature

The review of the literature is provided in a dissertation for a very specific reason. It presents to the reader the knowledge base upon which your study is built. This purpose reflects a time-honored tradition of scientific research: It acknowledges its indebtedness to the past and shows clear linkages between what was known in the past about the topic and what was discovered in the present research. This chapter explains one process you can use in writing an effective review of the literature.

As explained in previous chapters, the review of the literature usually constitutes Chapter 2 of the dissertation. In a smaller number of graduate schools, however, the student is encouraged to integrate the references to the literature throughout the dissertation, wherever appropriate, rather than writing a separate chapter. Be sure to check with your dissertation chair at the proposal defense. The following discussion assumes that you will have to write a separate chapter.

UPDATE THE COMPREHENSIVE CRITIQUE OF THE LITERATURE

The first step is to update your comprehensive critique of the literature. You want to be sure that your review is as current as you can make it. You should therefore do one more search of ERIC, requesting the most recent sources. You should check current issues of journals that publish educational research. You should use the Internet to contact other researchers working in your general field of study. You should also attend scholarly conferences and check conference programs so that you can send for papers that might not yet be published or entered into computerized databases.

REREAD ALL SOURCES

The next step is to reread all the usable sources that you have located. The purpose of this rereading is to freshen your understanding of what has been learned about the topic of your study. There are several systematic ways you can complete the rereading; the following method has worked effectively for many students. To clarify the process, the discussion assumes that the researcher is writing a review of the research on teachers' professional development.

1. Review each topical file. If you have followed the process explained in previous chapters, you have copies of all the sources filed in folders arranged topically. Take the first file and arrange the sources in order by date of publication. In the example used here, the first topical file might be "Stages of teachers' career development."

2. Identify each source with an appropriate code number, to simplify the way you refer to it in your own work. Thus, in the example used here, you might code the first article "Career stages 1."

3. Cross-reference sources appropriately. If one of the sources in a given topical file contains material

on another topic, make a simple note card for the second topical file reminding you of the source you should check. Suppose, for example, that the source "Career stages 1," which discusses "stages of teachers' career development," also contains usable material on "fostering teachers' development"; you would make a note card reading, "See Career stages 1" and add it to the "fostering" folder.

4. Reread each source and write a brief summary of it, to remind you of its main points and its perceived value to your review. Here is an example: "Stages 7. Huberman identifies 5 stages, each with a different theme. In Stages 3 and 4, the teacher may take one of two paths. Very useful review." Clip the summary to the source.

In this rereading process, put aside the following types of sources: opinions about current educational issues, reports of practice, and prescriptions of what should be done. Unless your chair advises you to the contrary, you should include only the theoretical literature and the empirical research.

DEVELOP THE FINAL OUTLINE

You should now be ready to develop the final outline. The first step in outlining involves identifying the major components of the literature review. You have several choices here, depending upon your own preferences and the requirements of the committee. Some reviews include an explanation of the search process that was used in assembling the review. Some reviews include a discussion of the theoretical literature. All include a review of the empirical research. Thus, there are four patterns frequently used.

Pattern 1

The search process

The theoretical literature

The empirical research

Pattern 2

The search process

The empirical research

Pattern 3

The theoretical literature

The empirical research

Pattern 4

The empirical research

As explained earlier, this matter should be resolved at the proposal defense, but you should check again with your dissertation chair as you get ready to write the chapter.

Now, take each major component and analyze it first to determine its own divisions. You do this by reflecting on this question: "What are the big pieces of this component?" If you have made wise choices in the way you have structured your files, then the way the files are organized can simplify this task for you. Here, for example, is how the researcher might identify the divisions of the component "methods of fostering teachers' professional development."

1. Supervision

2. Staff development

3. Graduate study

4. External workshops

5. Change in role

6. Change in teaching assignment

You may wish to note the subdivisions of divisions that are both complex and critical to the review. In the example given above, the division *Supervision* might be further analyzed in this manner:

1. Supervision
   a. Standard approaches
   b. Innovative approaches

The steps explained above should prepare you to write the final outline. Exhibit 15.1 shows the final outline for the review of the literature on teachers' professional

Exhibit 15.1   Outline, Teachers' Professional Development

I. Search process

II. Theoretical literature

   a. Jackson
   b. Burden
   c. Huberman

III. Empirical research

   a. Stages

      1. Entry
      2. Stabilization
      3. Experimentation/reassessment
      4. Serenity/conservatism
      5. Disengagement

   b. Factors influencing development

      1. Personal
      2. Contextual
      3. Intervention related

   c. Means of fostering professional development

      1. Supervision
      2. Staff development
      3. Graduate study
      4. External workshops
      5. Change in role
      6. Change in teaching assignment

development. Be sure to submit the final outline to your chair for his or her critique. You will spend a great deal of time writing the chapter, and you want to be sure that your time has not been wasted.

USE LEVELS OF HEADINGS THAT REFLECT THE OUTLINE

In all chapters, but especially in the review of the literature, use different levels of headings to reflect the outline and make clear to the reader how the chapter is organized. In most dissertations, four levels should be sufficient for clarity without getting too complex. Exhibit 15.2 shows how the four levels of headings can be used to reflect the outline shown in Exhibit 15.1; the heading style follows the recommendations of the *Publication Manual of the American Psychological Association* (6th ed.). The title of the chapter is considered Level 1; the main divisions of the chapter, Level 2; subdivisions, Level 3; and sub-subdivisions, Level 4.

WRITE THE INTRODUCTORY PARAGRAPH

The next step is to write the introduction to the chapter. Notice in Exhibit 15.2 that the introduction does not have its own heading. The introduction should be relatively brief, simply providing an overview of the chapter.

WRITE THE FIRST SECTION OF THE REVIEW

Now you should turn to the first section. In that first section—and in all succeeding ones—use this pattern: provide an overview, generalize, specify.

Exhibit 15.2   Headings, Teachers' Professional
                    Development

/level 1/   2. Review of the Literature

/intro/

A large body of literature on the nature of teachers' professional development provides a basis for the present study. This chapter will explain the search process in reviewing that literature and then examine both the theoretical and empirical studies in the field.

/level 2/   Search Process

The following review was developed through a systematic . . .

/level 2/   Theoretical Literature

Several theories have been advanced to explain the nature . . .

/level 2/   Empirical Research

The empirical studies that have been conducted have focused on three elements: the stages of development, factors influencing development, and means of fostering that development.

/level 3/   Stages of Development

Several major studies have examined teachers' professional development through the several stages of growth.

/level 4/   Entry stage

The entry stage, when the teachers begin their careers, is chiefly a time when the teacher develops survival skills.

Provide an Overview

Begin the first section with a brief overview, as shown in the first paragraph of Exhibit 15.3. (Exhibit 15.3 will be used to illustrate several of the points that follow.) The overview helps the reader understand how that section is organized and what its main divisions are.

Exhibit 15.3 Example of Review Style

Factors Influencing Teachers' Professional Development

Three groups of factors seem to influence teacher development: those involving the teacher as a person, those relating to the context, and those involving specific interventions. Those three factors interact in a complex manner, affecting each other and in turn influencing teacher development.

Personal Factors

Several personal elements seem to exercise a critical influence on the teacher's professional growth. Most researchers who have examined these personal elements have taken a developmental perspective on such aspects as the following: chronological age, ego development, moral development, career development, cognitive development, and motivational development. (See Burden, 1990, for a useful review.) Of all these personal factors, the ones that seem to play the most significant role are the teacher's cognitive development, career development, and motivational development. The research on these three factors will be discussed in the following sections.

Cognitive development. The teacher's cognitive development is usually equated with the extent to which the teacher can reason conceptually. Building upon David Hunt's work in conceptual development, Glickman (1981) posited three levels of abstract thinking—low, moderate, and high. Teachers at a low level think more concretely, would differentiate fewer concepts, and tend to see problems simplistically; those at a high level can reason abstractly, see connections between disparate elements, and enjoy complexity. Studies using conceptual level as the variable have concluded the following about teachers at the high level (as contrasted with those at the low level): They are more adaptable and flexible in teaching style, are more empathetic, provide more varied learning environments, are more tolerant of stress, are more effective with students of diverse ethnic backgrounds, and prefer to learn through a discovery model.

Although it would seem that one's cognitive level would be difficult to change, Sprinthall and Thies-Sprinthall (1983) provide evidence that cognitive development can be facilitated by

(Continued)

(Continued)

placing persons in significant role-taking situations (such as mentoring), along with continuous guided reflection and ongoing support.

Glickman's "developmental supervision" theory holds that supervisors working with teachers at a low level of conceptual development should be directive in their approach; with those at a moderate level, collaborative; and with those at a high level, nondirective. The research testing the effectiveness of such matching models seems inconclusive.

Career development. The term *career development* is used here to denote the growth experienced as teachers move through the stages of their professional careers. Several researchers have investigated the patterns of growth and stagnation that emerge as teachers remain in the profession, each using different terms to identify the stages. The conceptualization that seems to be the most rigorous in its formulation is that advanced by Huberman and his colleagues (1989). (See also Huberman's 1989 article for a summary of the research.)

Huberman's synthesis of the theory and research on career development posits five stages of the professional career, demarcated in terms of years of teaching experience. *Career entry,* from the first to the third year, is a time of both survival and discovery; the survival theme is the one most often sounded in studies of beginning teachers. At the same time, many report a sense of discovery, as they work with their own pupils and become part of a collegial group. Those with from four to six years of teaching experience seem then to move into a *stabilization* period, when tenure is granted, a definitive commitment to the career of teaching is made, and a sense of instructional mastery is achieved. Those with from seven to eighteen years of experience seem to diverge. Some teachers report this period as one of experimentation and activism, when they try out new approaches, develop their own courses, and confront institutional barriers. Other teachers report this period as one of self-doubt and reassessment, when disenchantment with the system leads many to consider changing professions.

Divergence also occurs during the period between nineteen and thirty years of experience. For many it is a time of relaxed self-acceptance and serenity, accompanied by a developing awareness of greater relational distance from their pupils. For many other teachers this period is one of conservatism; these teachers seem to complain a great deal, criticizing the administrators, their colleagues, and their students. The final period, from thirty-one to forty years of teaching experience, is a stage of disengagement, a gradual withdrawal as the end of the career looms; for some it is a time of serenity; for others, a time of bitterness.

Level of motivation. The third personal factor is the teacher's level of motivation—defined here as the strength of the inner drive to achieve professional goals. Glatthorn (1990) has identified several factors that, according to a significant body of research, influence the teacher's motivational level. The first is a supportive environment, which includes five features: relationships with students and parents are positive, effective leadership is present, the physical conditions are adequate, the school climate is positive, and the teacher has a manageable teaching assignment. The second motivating factor is meaningful work: The teacher has an appropriate degree of autonomy, and the teacher believes in the significance of the work.

The third factor is the teacher's belief system. The following beliefs are essential for a high level of motivation: I can perform successfully; the actions I take will achieve the results I want; those results will be recognized by rewards that I value. The fourth factor in motivation is the teacher's goals. The teacher's level of motivation is more likely to be high when the teacher's goals are shared by peers, when the goal-setting process is a collaborative one, when the goals are specific, and when the goals are challenging but attainable.

Next, the rewards are significant. A teacher's level of motivation is more likely to increase when more emphasis is placed on such intrinsic rewards as a sense of competence and a feeling of accomplishment and when student achievement is emphasized as a meaningful reward. The research in general concludes that teachers are more

(Continued)

(Continued)

motivated by such intrinsic rewards as the satisfaction of improving learning than they are by extrinsic ones such as merit pay (Dilworth, 1991). It should be noted here, however, that there may be some national differences in the power of intrinsic elements. A comparison of the attitudes of teachers in France and England concluded that inner-city French teachers are much less likely to perceive teaching as a means of giving meaning to life and are far more likely to see it simply as a means of earning a living (Broadfoot & Osborn, 1987).

The final factor in teacher motivation is the type and frequency of feedback. Several studies suggest that the teacher's level of motivation is more likely to increase when the teacher makes continuing assessments of student learning and uses positive results as reinforcement. In addition, frequent and positive feedback from administrators and supervisors can also increase the level of teacher motivation.

Contextual Factors

The contextual factors, as construed here, are all those elements of the environment that impact teacher development. The context is perceived broadly, including what McLaughlin and Talbert (1990) term *five embedded contextual layers*.

Generalize

Then write the main developmental paragraphs of that section. Ordinarily you should begin the developmental paragraphs with one or two sentences that generalize what the studies show, as Exhibit 15.3 indicates. Less skilled writers simply enumerate the conclusions of each study, something like this:

Cashwell (2005) concluded that staff development programs are not effective. Stroud (2007) concluded that they can be effective if certain conditions hold true. Shew (2008) concluded that coaching was an important condition of all successful programs.

The point being made here is that you have an obligation to the reader to make coherent sense of the literature, instead of simply describing it.

Specific Reminders

With the generalization made, you then provide the specific evidence, citing and discussing each study relating to that generalization. How much space you devote to each study depends upon its importance. A major study should be treated at length, requiring one to four manuscript pages. A study of moderate significance for your own research can be treated in several paragraphs. A less important study might simply be noted as one of several sources or be discussed briefly in one paragraph. Just be sure that the length of treatment corresponds to importance.

WRITE THE REMAINING SECTIONS, INCLUDING A SUMMARY

Use the same pattern of providing an overview, generalizing, and specifying when writing the remainder of the sections. Conclude the chapter with a summary, probably a page or two in length, which reviews the content of the chapter and brings together the key conclusions of all the empirical research.

Specific Reminders

As you write the chapter, keep in mind some specific suggestions made previously:

- Vary the way you refer to studies. Notice in the example in Exhibit 15.3 that the author uses several techniques.

- Paraphrase; do not quote. Quote directly only when it seems important to preserve the words of the original.
- Be sure each section is organized clearly and gives the reader verbal signals that indicate organization.
- Use headings that reveal the organizational pattern.

Evaluate and Revise

When you have finished writing the chapter, put it aside for a while. Then revise it, using such technological aids as spell checkers, a thesaurus, and style checkers. You should also find the criteria listed in Exhibit 15.4 helpful in the revision process.

Exhibit 15.4 Criteria: Literature Review

Is the review . . .

1. Comprehensive, including all major works relating to your topic?

2. In depth, providing the reader depth of knowledge about the prior research?

3. Current, including works published recently?

4. Selective, discriminating between major and less important studies?

5. Unbiased, without the writer skewing the prior research to suit his or her point of view?

6. Clearly organized, so that the reader can easily follow the plan and flow of the chapter?

7. Coherent, making sense of the studies, not simply describing them?

8. Effectively written, with a scholarly style?

TECHNOLOGY TECHNIQUE: FORMATTING QUOTES

For formatting quotes, two techniques depend on the length of the quote. If the quotation is composed of less than 40 words, the quote is included in the text using quotation marks. If the quote has 40 or more words, the quote must be formatted in block text without quotation marks. A good way to determine the word count is to use the word count function within your word processing tools program.

SIXTEEN

Explaining the Methodology

You should be able to write the methodology chapter without a great deal of difficulty, if you have kept careful records. This chapter will explain what steps to take and what content to include in this chapter.

PREPARE TO WRITE THE CHAPTER

In preparing to write the chapter, you can take several steps. First, you should reread Chapters 5 and 9 of this work. They both provide some helpful suggestions about the methodology. Second, review your records. Your researcher's journal should be especially useful. Finally, review your results; they will remind you of what methods you have used.

USE AN OBJECTIVE STYLE IN WRITING THE CHAPTER

Objectivity is especially important in this chapter. In describing the research site, avoid making unsupported judgments, sweeping generalizations, and extreme statements. Instead, provide specific data, noting just the facts as you recorded them. Contrast these two versions.

TOO SUBJECTIVE: The school building looked as if a disaster had hit it. Nobody cared about the place or wanted to improve it. It was a terrible environment for learning.

MORE OBJECTIVE: The overall appearance of the building suggested that it was not well maintained. Custodian Walker (a fictitious name) apologized for the appearance, noting that his staff had been cut. He noted that in early October he had reported to the head of facilities that the roof of the gym leaked, but by March when this study took place, nothing had been done.

In achieving specificity and objectivity, you may find it helpful to present much of the data in table form. If you do, be sure to use the specified style guide format adopted by the institution conferring the degree. Remember that the table is used to present data, with the accompanying text used to comment on the highlights, not simply repeat what is in the table.

DETERMINE THE CONTENT OF THE CHAPTER

With these preparatory steps accomplished, you should turn next to developing an outline of the chapter. To do so, you first need to determine the content of the chapter. Obviously this will vary with the methods you have used and the steps you have taken. Most descriptions of methodology will include the following content: the general research perspective and research type; the research context, including a specification of time and place; the research participants; the instruments used in data collection; the procedures used in collecting the data; and the way you analyzed the data. A chapter summary is also typically included.

OUTLINE THE CHAPTER AND USE HEADINGS APPROPRIATELY

Now you are ready to develop the outline itself and use the outline to determine the headings you will use.

Make an Outline

When you have decided on content, you then should determine the overall organizational pattern. Four patterns are commonly found in dissertations, as follows:

Logical Order. Most chapters will use a logical order, organizing the content in terms of the relationships of the concepts. Such an order is shown in Exhibit 16.1. You reflect on the processes you used and determine how best to group them.

The logical order shown in Exhibit 16.1 will be used to organize the discussion that follows, since it includes most of the elements included in the methodology chapter.

Chronological Order. Some researchers using a qualitative or action research approach prefer to follow a chronological order, discussing the steps in the order in which they were taken. This pattern is especially useful when the sequence of steps is important to the result.

Research-Question Order. Another organizational pattern frequently used in dissertations is to explain the methodology in relation to the research questions answered. Consider this example. The researcher studying teachers' planning as it related to curriculum standards posed these three specific questions:

Exhibit 16.1 Example of Methodology Chapter

3. Methodology

This chapter explains the methods used in completing the study, giving special emphasis to the analysis of data. It should be noted at the outset that the methodology to a certain extent was an evolving one, which took definite shape as the study progressed.

The General Perspective

As a qualitative study, the research reported here embodies both quantitative and qualitative perspectives . . .

The Research Context

The study took place in a charter school in its first year of operation. For purposes of confidentiality, the school will be referred to with the fictitious name . . .

The Research Participants

Although the researcher was inevitably aware of the actions of both the director and the students, his primary concern was with the actions of the teachers. . . .

Instruments Used in Data Collection

Several instruments and recording processes were used in the data collection process. First, . . .

Procedures Used

In completing the research design, several specific procedures were used. . . .

Data Analysis

The data were analyzed using several strategies. First, the data were reduced by . . .

Summary of the Methodology

To summarize the previous explanation, it should be emphasized that the study used both . . .

Question 1. To what extent are teachers familiar with curriculum standards?

Question 2. To what extent do teachers use curriculum standards in making yearly plans?

Question 3. To what extent are teachers conscious of using curriculum standards as they teach?

The researcher used those three questions to organize the methodology chapter, using the simple outline shown in Exhibit 16.2.

Research Methods Order. Finally, you may find that organizing the chapter in relation to the research methods makes the most sense. Thus, you might have sections identified as follows: observation methods, interview methods, survey methods.

Common Elements. Regardless of the organizational pattern used, two initial elements are common to most dissertations: the general perspective and the research context. The reader would also expect to find an introductory paragraph and a summary.

Once you have developed an outline, submit it to your chair for review.

Exhibit 16.2   Outline by Question

1. General research perspective and type

2. Research context and participants

3. Methods used for Question 1

4. Methods used for Question 2

5. Methods used for Question 3

6. Summary

Use Appropriate Headings

When the chair has approved the outline, be sure to use headings that will reflect the outline and make it clear to the reader. Note that the headings shown in Exhibit 16.1 use only Level 1, for the chapter title, and Level 2, for the main divisions. You may see a need to use Level 3 to identify subdivisions under the Level 2 headings.

DESCRIBE THE CONTEXT FOR THE STUDY

The term *context* is used to identify the place and time of the study. A detailed description of the research site will enable other researchers and readers to better understand the findings. Depending on the nature of your study, you can choose to describe one or more of the following levels:

- State department and the regional service center
- School district or school system
- School
- Classroom or other special location
- Community

Which aspects do you include in your description? The answer is, all those that the reader needs to understand the specialness of the research context. Exhibit 16.3 lists most of the aspects that might be included for school district, school, classroom, and community—the contexts most often used in educational research. Do not use that list as a prescription; use it instead as a set of guidelines designed to help you decide what to include.

In most dissertations, you should give these entities fictitious names to preserve confidentiality. Indicate that the name is fictitious the first time you use it. This is one way you can do so: "Lincoln High School is a large grades 9 through 12 high school in a major city in the East. (Lincoln is a fictitious name, used to preserve confidentiality.)"

Exhibit 16.3 Aspects of the Research Site

School district

1. Attendance areas included
2. District organizational structure
3. School board composition and stability
4. Central office staff, including leaders and their tenure
5. Number of students served
6. Grade level organization
7. Number of schools at each level
8. Ethnic composition of student body
9. Number and nature of professional staff
10. Overall student achievement
11. Recent reform activities
12. General nature of parent relationships

School

1. Attendance area
2. Leadership structure and organization
3. Grade levels and student enrollment
4. Student demographics, ethnicity, and nature of special population
5. Special features of educational programs and curriculum
6. Composition of certified and support staff
7. Testing program
8. Student achievement results
9. Attendance rates
10. Suspension and retention rates
11. Physical condition and appearance of facilities
12. Major concerns and problems
13. Recent reform efforts

Classroom

1. Size, location, physical appearance
2. Student composition: social class, ethnicity, gender, ability

3. Teacher and support staff: attendance, education, experience, gender, ethnicity

4. Student achievement

5. Student attendance and promptness

6. Equipment and materials

7. Curriculum

Community

1. Area covered and general nature of community (urban, suburban, rural)

2. Population: socioeconomic level, ethnicity, political affiliation, population trends

3. Tax base and economic stability

4. Businesses, industries, and social services

5. Major community strengths and problems

In describing the context, be sure to indicate as well the time period for the study, perhaps in this manner: "The research activities covered a two-month period, from March 1, 1999, to May 30, 1999."

IDENTIFY THE SUBJECTS OR PARTICIPANTS

You also need to provide specific information about all those who participated in the study. In most quantitative studies they are identified as *subjects;* in most qualitative studies, as participants. In either case, provide the specific information the reader will need to understand the study. In most quantitative studies, you will need to provide descriptive statistics such as number, age, ethnic identity, and gender, usually presented in a table. In qualitative studies the reader expects to find more detailed descriptions of the participants, as in this example:

Harrison Peel has been teaching English for 30 years. Educated at an Ivy League school and with a master's degree in Renaissance literature, he prides himself on his love of literature. Once married to a woman whom he always describes in generous terms, he is now widowed, and lives by himself in a small apartment in downtown Centreville. He is a slight man in physical appearance, but as far as this researcher could determine, he never seems to have any trouble controlling even potentially disruptive students. He speaks with a clear, strong voice even when conversing with colleagues. . . .

In quantitative studies, the reader will expect to find details about the selection process, including the following issues: From which population were they selected? What sampling procedure was used, if any? How were they assigned to groups? What previous experience did they have with the content, the instruments, the intervention, or the personnel?

IDENTIFY THE INSTRUMENTS USED TO COLLECT DATA

A key part of the methodology is the instrumentation used to collect data. The term *instrumentation* is a general one that includes the following:

OBSERVATION INSTRUMENTS: Observation forms, observation guidelines, observation schedules

INTERVIEWS: Interview protocols (questions to be asked), interview recording devices, interview guidelines

SURVEYS: Survey forms, survey directions

DOCUMENT ANALYSIS: Document analysis guidelines, criteria

TESTS AND MEASUREMENTS: Tests used, performance assessment tasks, measurement guidelines

If you used an existing instrument, you should report on its validity and reliability. If it was an instrument for which you had to secure permission, include in an appendix the letter giving you permission. If you developed your own instrument, the reader will expect to find an explanation of how you developed it, including how you tested for validity and reliability and what results you obtained. Copies of any instruments you have developed should be included in the appendix.

EXPLAIN THE PROCEDURES USED IN COMPLETING THE DESIGN

Now you explain in a step-by-step manner what procedures you used in completing the design. The procedures followed would obviously vary with the type of research. In the standard experimental study, you would probably identify these steps:

1. Access confirmed

2. Subjects randomly assigned to experimental and control groups

3. Both groups given a pretest

4. Experimental group given the treatment; control group received no treatment

5. Both groups given posttest

On the other hand, an action research study explaining how a team solved a problem might report the procedures under two main headings:

1. Procedures the team used in solving the problem

2. Procedures the researcher used in studying the team's processes

Regardless of the type of study, you are required to explain the procedures in sufficient detail for two key reasons. First, doing so enables other researchers to replicate the study. Second, doing so enables potential consumers to determine if your findings can be trusted.

EXPLAIN HOW THE DATA WERE ANALYZED

All studies will result in a mass of raw data. Thus, a key component of the methodology chapter is explaining to the reader how you handled those data. The data analysis usually includes three procedures.

First, you explain how you reduced the data. When you reduce the data, you group the raw data to make initial sense of them. In analyzing interview data, for example, a student researcher reported these steps in reducing the data:

1. Transcribing the interviews

2. Reading the transcripts to tentatively identify categories of responses

3. Testing the tentative categories by classifying responses in the first hour of the interviews

4. Using final categories to code all responses

5. Tallying coded responses

Next, you explain how you decided to report and display the reduced data. You have several choices of reporting methods: raw data, percentages, mean, median, or standardized scores. You also have several methods for displaying data: narrative text, matrix, tables, graphs, charts, or other figures.

Finally, you explain how you analyzed those data to determine what they meant. In quantitative studies, you report the statistical tests and procedures used; in qualitative studies, you explain how you interpreted the data.

WRITE A SUMMARY

The final step is to write a brief summary that highlights the key features of the methodology and looks ahead to the next chapter. Here is one example:

> This chapter has explained the methods used in this qualitative study of one school's attempt to use performance assessments. The next chapter presents the results obtained with those methods.

TECHNOLOGY TECHNIQUE: FORMATTING

Educational institutions that grant graduate degrees adopt a style manual for graduate students to use in preparing formal papers such as dissertations. A style manual, such as the *Publication Manual of the American Psychological Association,* describes the appearance (format) of the components of a formal paper. Although most colleges and universities adopt the style manual in its entirety, some modify the guidelines for components of the document (i.e., the title page). For example, one southern university requires a two-page title page; however, when numbering those pages, the two-page title page is counted as one page—the page numbering may be a modification from the style manual. Any special university requirements supersede the style manual guidelines.

A particularly troublesome aspect in a dissertation is the use of headings and the appearance or format of those headings. For graduate students who write the document and for university administrators who review the completed approved dissertation, interpreting the style manual guidelines is a challenge and may lead to unneeded frustration. Furthermore, the names of the levels of headings differ in various style manuals, which again may lead to confused writers.

To avoid this unneeded confusion and frustration, submit a completed chapter to your chair. During the conference with your chair after his or her review, talk about the headings and obtain his or her opinions on them. If your chair is not certain about the format or appearance of the headings, ask for help in arranging an appointment with a university administrator who typically reviews dissertations for the university.

By being proactive in the early stages of writing the dissertation, you will save time in the university approval process. In addition, your anxiety toward the university approval process will be reduced.

SEVENTEEN

Presenting the Results

In most dissertations, the results of the data analyses are presented in a separate chapter—the fourth chapter. In some qualitative studies, the results are reported in detail in two or three chapters. Regardless of tho number of chapters, there are certain strategies you can use.

PREPARE TO PRESENT THE RESULTS

Before turning to issues of organization and writing, you should take two preparatory steps. First, review the results carefully. If you used a statistical package for data analyses, repeat the analyses to verify the accuracy. Second, check the style guide for the format of tables and figures if you plan to present some of your data in these formats.

DECIDE ON THE CONTENTS AND FORMAT OF THE CHAPTER

In the initial planning process, review your data and decide the following content and format issues:

- What will be included in the appendix of the dissertation? These materials are typically included in the appendices: instructions to participants, questionnaires and survey forms, copies of instruments used, and letters of access and permission.
- What will be included in tables? In general, tables are used to present complex data in columns and rows. Tables are useful since they present multiple data in a form easy to understand. As the APA *Publication Manual* notes, however, they also have two disadvantages: too many tables distract the reader and complicate the processing of text.
- What figures will be needed? A figure is any illustration other than a table; the term *figure* includes graphs, photographs, and line drawings. Figures are especially useful in showing nonlinear relationships. A figure should be easy to read and should complement, not duplicate, the text.

In determining the contents of this chapter, you do not need to interpret the data—present only your analysis or analyses as well as any resulting statistical significance or nonsignificance if applicable. Your last chapter will typically include a summary and a discussion. In most dissertations the "discussion" section is the best place for interpretation. If you include interpretation in the "results" chapter, you will not have much new to say in the final chapter, which may be the more important chapter for the reader.

Determine the Organization of the Chapter

Your decisions about content and format will simplify the development of your outline for the chapter. As with the methodology, you have several choices about the order to use:

- By hypotheses. If your study involves research or null hypotheses, you may decide to order by hypothesis: Hypothesis 1, Hypothesis 2, and so on.
- By research question. If your study involved two or more specific research questions, then ordering in terms of those questions would be useful: Question 1, Question 2, and so on.
- By research method. If you used multiple methods, grouping the results in relation to the methods may be helpful: interview results, survey results, and so on.
- By chronology. If the time order is important, then organize by chronology: entry, middle phase, and exiting. You can also use a chronological pattern in studies that relied chiefly on testing: pretest results, followed by posttest results.
- By variable. If the variables are critical to the study, then order by variable, such as age, self-concept, and achievement level.

Obviously several patterns can work. One way of deciding is to reflect in this manner: "I stated the problem in Chapter 1; I explained my methodology in Chapter 3; I will summarize in Chapter 5. How can I best take my reader from Chapter 3 to Chapter 5?" Also, keep in mind the advantages of consistency. If readers find three null hypotheses in Chapter 1, and then discover in Chapter 3 that the methodology was presented in relation to those three null hypotheses, they will expect to find the three null hypotheses governing the reporting of results. However, keep in mind that first-person personal pronouns should be avoided, especially in quantitative studies.

Submit your outline to the dissertation chair and make any revisions necessary. Remember that you should always write from an approved outline; doing so will avoid much unnecessary revision.

DEVELOP THE TABLES AND FIGURES

Before you begin to write the text of the Results or Analysis/Analyses of Data chapter, create all the tables and figures that you will need. While it is possible to make the tables and figures as you write the text, you should find it simpler to make them first, since doing so will simplify the writing task. The APA *Publication Manual* (2010) offers several questions to help you make effective tables, paraphrased as follows:

1. Is the table essential?

2. Is the entire table double-spaced?

3. Is the title brief but clear?

4. Does every column have a column heading?

5. Are all abbreviations and symbols explained?

6. Are notes presented in proper form and order?

Figures also should meet specific criteria: They supplement without duplicating the text; they convey only the essential facts, omitting distracting information; they are easy to read and understand.

WRITE THE INTRODUCTORY PARAGRAPH

In writing the introductory paragraph of this chapter, you might find it useful to begin with a sentence that restates the problem, simply to remind the reader. Then follow with a sentence that provides an overview of the chapter. Here is an example:

As stated in Chapter 1, the study examined the problems encountered by teachers as they developed and used performance assessments in their planning and teaching. This chapter is organized in terms of the three null hypotheses presented in Chapter 1. The

study first examined the problems teachers encountered in developing performance assessments; it
then inspected the difficulties they experienced in
using those assessments in their teaching. Finally, the
need for training to use the results of such performance assessments was addressed.

WRITE THE FIRST SECTION

In general, you will find that this pattern works in writing
each section. First, state a generalization that summarizes the results. Then refer to any table or figure that you
have developed. Finally, provide the specific evidence.
Here is an example, using the contrived table shown in
Exhibit 17.1.

Note that the narrative text does not simply rehash the
information presented in the table. Instead, it calls attention
to the major findings. The writer assumes that the reader
can locate in the table all the specific data needed.

In writing this and succeeding sections, remember the
importance of objectivity. Report the results without interpreting them or using modifiers that imply a point of view.

WRITE THE REMAINING SECTIONS, USING APPROPRIATE HEADINGS

Use that same pattern in writing the remaining sections.
Remember to use the appropriate levels of headings to
clarify the organization of the chapter. When you have
finished writing the main sections of the chapter, write a
brief concluding paragraph that notes generally what you
have discovered and points the reader to the following
chapter. Here is an example:

The results presented above indicate clearly that the
teachers in this study experienced greatest difficulty
in using performance assessments as a basis for

Exhibit 17.1

Primary Sources Used

Teachers in 2007 have changed in the primary source used in making long-term plans, compared with their counterparts in 1986. As indicated in Table 1, more of the 2007 teachers are using the state test as a guide, and fewer are relying upon the textbook and their own knowledge of students. (See Table 1.)

Example of Table

Table 1   Primary Source Used for Developing Long-Term Plans for Instruction

Primary Source	1997 %	1986 %
District curriculum guide	12	8
State test	24	12
Textbook	18	26
Teacher's knowledge of students	22	32
Suggestions by colleagues	13	15
Plans from previous year	9	6
Other	3	2

Note: Totals do not equal 100 because of rounding.

their teaching. A more detailed summary and a discussion of the findings are presented in the next chapter.

REVISE THE CHAPTER AND SUBMIT IT FOR REVIEW

In revising the chapter, keep in mind the criteria listed in Exhibit 17.2. They will remind you of the key characteristics

Exhibit 17.2   Criteria: Presenting the Results

Does the presentation of results . . .

1. Use an appropriate organizational pattern and make that pattern clear to the reader?

2. Report results accurately and objectively?

3. Effectively integrate text with tables and figures, without unnecessary repetition?

4. Use format for tables and figures as specified by the style manual?

5. Emphasize results, without excessive interpretation and discussion?

desired in this chapter. When you have finished your own revision, submit it to your dissertation chair for his or her review.

TECHNOLOGY TECHNIQUE: USING SOFTWARE TO CREATE FIGURES AND TABLES

For formal papers such as dissertations and theses, tables and figures are a necessity. Tables and figures are an easy approach to presenting information in a format that is easily understood by the reader. For the author, tables and figures can be a nightmare to create and format. With today's software—both word processing and spreadsheet—the creation of tables is simpler. But the author needs to be familiar with the software and the "ins and outs" of such software to use it effectively and efficiently. Otherwise, the author may experience extreme frustration with the software. Both word processing and spreadsheet software allow the creation of tables; consequently, the author must decide which one is the optimum for his or her use.

To use this option, the author needs to know the number of columns and rows in a table. Thus, prior to creating the table using the word processing or spreadsheet software, a "hard copy, paper, draft" version of the table needs to be prepared. At some point in the process, the title for the table should be considered because the number of lines used for the title impacts the creation of the table. For example, the sixth edition of the *Publication Manual of the American Psychological Association* (APA, 2010, p. 129) specifies at least two lines for the table title: Table Number and Table Title. By generating a hard copy draft version, the author easily can determine the number of columns and rows needed for the title block as well as the entire table. When determining the number of rows, any footnote lines need to be considered.

Word processing software, such as Microsoft Word, has a "Table" option; this option may be found as a separate menu item or it may be a submenu. The location of the Table option in Microsoft Word depends on the version of the software. In Microsoft Word 2010, the Table menu item is found as a submenu under the Insert tab on the ribbon at the top of the screen. When examining the submenu for "Tables," an author may see several options. The available options may be used, but their use should be limited if the author is not familiar with the capability of the option choices. It is in the best interest of the author to revise the table format prior to creating the table in the word processing software.

Spreadsheet software, such as Microsoft Excel, is a giant table composed of rows and columns; spreadsheet software is ideal for those users who are comfortable with creating a table at the computer. The author inputs the information for the table and uses the insert line or column feature to add rows or columns when needed for data that were not considered earlier. When the table is finished, use the spreadsheet software's "cut and paste" or "copy and paste" features to move the table from the spreadsheet document to the word processing document. A word of caution: Be certain that the font and point size are the same in both the word processing and spreadsheet software; if you do not, reformatting for the font and point size will be necessary.

Thus, the author should base his or her use of the Table alternatives in either the word processing or spreadsheet software on his or her knowledge of the software and his or her comfort level with using such technology. Otherwise, entering the information into the word processing software to create the table will be challenging and create unneeded frustration. The end result is a usable table when either word processing or spreadsheet software is used. The process used to create the table is not important—the readability and understanding of the information contained within the table is the critical element: Focus more on the information than the process!

EIGHTEEN

Summarizing and Discussing the Results

The last chapter of the dissertation is commonly titled *Summary and Discussion.* An older style uses the title *Conclusions and Recommendations.* The title presently used seems more accurate, however, since many studies include neither conclusions nor recommendations.

REVIEW THE RESULTS REPORTED

Begin by reviewing the results of your study. While the previous chapter reported the results in detail, the last chapter reports the general findings. You, therefore, should review the Data Analyses/Results chapter to identify the general results that should be included in the final chapter. If you have written the Results chapter in the general-to-specific pattern recommended in this book, you should be able to identify the general results with minimal difficulty.

Develop an Outline of the Final Chapter

The outline of the final chapter is different from those for preceding chapters. Since many readers will review and read first the last chapter of your dissertation, you should write it so that it tells the full story of your study. This means that it should include five main parts, as follows:

1. Introduction

2. Statement of the problem

3. Review of the methodology

4. Summary of the results

5. Discussion of the results

In developing an outline for your chair to review, you should provide additional detail for both the summary and the discussion. For example, the outline for the discussion section might look like this:

1. Interpretation of the findings

2. Relationship of the current study to previous research

3. Recommendations for educators

4. Suggestions for additional research

When you have drafted the outline, submit it to your dissertation chair for review.

Write the Introductory Paragraph

The introductory paragraph, like those for previous chapters, should be brief; it should also be presented without a heading. Here is an example of what might be said:

As previously mentioned, this study was conducted to explore the relationship between teacher planning and student performance on state-mandated tests. The final chapter of the dissertation restates the research problem and reviews the major methods used in the study. The major sections of this chapter summarize the results and discuss their implications.

RESTATE THE PROBLEM AND REVIEW THE METHODOLOGY

Next, present the problem statement exactly as it appears in Chapter 1. Then review the methodology in sufficient detail, without excessive repetition. Here is an example to illustrate the level of generality:

> As explained in Chapter 2, the research was a case study of a principal newly appointed as a replacement for a principal who had been relieved of his duties because of the school's low performance on state mandated tests. As a case study, this research primarily used a qualitative perspective, attempting to discern the meaning of events to the participants. The case study covered the new principal's initial five months at the school.
>
> The case study relied chiefly on observations and interviews. The researcher observed the principal for nineteen Thursdays, in each instance spending six hours observing the principal in action. Each observation was followed by a debriefing interview; five general interviews were also held, one each month. Four teachers identified by their colleagues as key informants were interviewed on the same day as the general principal interview.

Observe that that review of the methodology provides sufficient information for a reader who has not read the detailed methodology chapter to understand how the study was conducted.

SUMMARIZE THE RESULTS

In summarizing the results, keep in mind the importance of interchapter consistency. For most dissertations, the statement of the problem in Chapter 1, the review of related literature in Chapter 2, the explanation of the methodology in Chapter 3, the presentation of the results in Chapter 4, and the summary of the results in Chapter 5 should be organized in a consistent manner. However, any organization of the summary that is approved by your chair and that makes sense to the reader will suffice.

You should find that the general-to-specific pattern works well in summarizing the results: Begin with the general statement and then support it with appropriate details. Here is an example:

> Throughout the entire period of the study, Principal Turlington used a style of leadership that she considered effective but that seemed to confuse the teachers. In all the general interviews, Turlington characterized her style as "flexible" and repeatedly assured the researcher that the school needed a leader who knew how to adjust—to "go with the flow," as she put it. However, the teachers interviewed saw her style differently. In their interviews they frequently used terms such as "inconsistent," "uncertain," and "wishy-washy." In contrasting Turlington's leadership style with that of her predecessor, one teacher commented, "With Carpenter, you always knew where you stood; with Turlington, you are never quite sure." Similar sentiments were expressed by three other informants.

Note that the paragraph above begins with a general statement, followed by supporting evidence. However, the supporting evidence is limited to a few relevant spe-cifics; the writer does not wish to present all the details just reported in the previous chapter.

Observe as well that the writer couches the summary in objective language, for the most part avoiding interpre-tations. Where interpretations are made, the writer uses the word *seems* to indicate tentativeness. Although it is often difficult to separate observations from interpreta-tions, you should do all you can to save the interpretive language for the Discussion section.

Finally, increase the clarity of the summary section by using appropriate transitional cues. You can use sequencing words, such as *first, also, next,* and *finally.* You can number the general findings in this manner:

1. Students in the experimental group expressed strong dissatisfaction with their insufficient face-to-face contact with the distance instructor.

You can also use bullets to highlight your findings, as in this example:

- Higher levels of student achievement were associ-ated with higher scores on the Index of Community.

DISCUSS THE MEANING OF THE STUDY

The Discussion section of the final dissertation chapter is probably the most crucial section of all. Evidence of its importance is the fact that in many scientific reports the discussion of the findings amounts to one-third of the entire report. Many readers will read only this section since they want to know only what the study means. The discussion is also your opportunity to bring yourself into the document. Although you are still expected to deal with the facts of your study, your readers will expect to hear more of your own voice as you try to make sense of the findings.

Reflect on Your Findings

The process should begin with a time of reflection. One useful way of reflecting is to imagine that you are standing before an audience of your peers. A questioner asks, "Well, aside from all those details, what does your study mean?" Think about the answer you would give if you had only five minutes to respond. The ideas that come to you in this time of reflection should help you consider the content of this section.

Determine the Content of the Discussion Section

As indicated previously, you should have developed an outline for the entire chapter. If you have not already done so, you should determine the specific content of this section. Although each discussion will vary, certain common elements are frequently found.

Researcher's Insights. The reader expects you to make sense of the study, since you were deeply involved in the research. Your interpretations, however, should avoid sounding too dogmatic. Here is an example of the tone you are trying to achieve:

> On the basis of this study alone, it is difficult to be certain about the factors accounting for Turlington's seeming lack of consistency in style. As noted above, she ascribed it to a desire to be flexible. However, subtle signs existed that suggested her predecessor's rigidity may have been a contributing factor.

> Research by Womble (2002) indicates that a replacement principal hired during the school year will frequently seem tentative in dealing with a faculty as the newly hired principal is an unknown . . .

Relationship of the Current Study to Prior Research. You are also expected to relate your findings to previous research. As indicated in the example given above, you may indicate this relationship as you interpret the findings. You may also deal with it in a separate subsection, with its own heading. The key issue is to show clearly to the reader how your study builds upon the knowledge base. Here is an example:

> Previous studies (Clemens, 1999; Lewis, 2000; Rivers, 1998) of effective principals have concluded that they were especially assertive in their dealings with the faculty during the first semester of their tenure as principal.

> The present study yields a very different portrait of a principal during the "honeymoon" period.

Theoretical Implications of the Study. It well may be that your study has some major theoretical implications: It may confirm existing theory or present disconfirming evidence. If it does, then you should call attention to these implications, as in this example:

> Cashwell's (1997) theory of the "zone of acceptance" would have predicted that these teachers would have been receptive to Turlington's decisions in areas where they had no personal stake. However, the teachers in this study frequently manifested resistance even when the decisions had no immediate impact on them. . . .

Explanation of Unanticipated Findings. If the results of your study seemed unanticipated or surprising, the reader expects an explanation. The types of factors you might consider are problems with the research design, the use of an exceptional population, sampling errors, mistakes in the control of variables, defects in the instrument, or poor implementation of the treatment. In explaining the unanticipated results, do not apologize for yourself or blame others; simply note the problem. Here is an example of the appropriate tone:

> The fact that the experimental group did not show gains that were statistically significant may have resulted from the teachers' failure to implement the new approach as it had been designed. Discussions with the teachers after the treatment had been implemented indicated that there were major differences in the way the trainers had presented the new unit to the teachers. . . .

Implications for Practice. Many educational studies will have clear implications for practice. Although you should feel free to make such recommendations, you should again avoid making dogmatic assertions or sweeping recommendations that go far beyond your study. Here is an example of an appropriate way of making effective recommendations:

> Although a single case study cannot provide a sound basis for the practice of leadership, this study (and other case studies with similar findings) would suggest that newly appointed principals should understand that most faculty in such a context expect changes to be made during the first months of incumbency. . . .

Recommendations for Further Research. Finally, you should decide if you should include in this final chapter your recommendations for additional research. If you do so, note only the research that your own study suggests is needed. Some student researchers make the mistake of simply listing an array of interesting topics, many of which have no relationship to their study. Here is how you might accomplish this purpose:

Additional research seems needed on the principal expectations by faculty. As noted above, it is possible that the faculty expectations of the principal was a factor in Turlington's seeming lack of consistency. Although there have been a few studies of this issue, there is no consistent evidence. . . .

Write the Discussion Section

In writing the Discussion section, do not feel that you have to follow a prescribed order. This section is one place where interchapter consistency is not critical. Tell your story in any way that seems effective. Feel free to be somewhat more subjective.

TECHNOLOGY TECHNIQUE: SOFTWARE CAPABILITIES

Regardless of the software used in the preparation of the dissertation—word processing, spreadsheet, reference, and so on—you, the author, should understand that the software programs used are only tools. The successful use of these tools depends on the author's ability to use them effectively. If you are technology literate, as most graduate students are today, then taking advantage of the capability of these tools is to your advantage. However, if you are not familiar with technology, then you may be limited in what you can do on your own; you may want to consider securing an individual who is familiar with the software as well as with the institution conferring the degree submission requirements to format the final document. Because the final document is perceived as a reflection of you and your work, you want it to be the best. Furthermore, using an individual who is familiar with the "in's and out's" of the university's requirements will reduce your frustrations at this stage and move you close to a "done dissertation" that is a "winning dissertation."

IV

Defending and Profiting From the Dissertation

NINETEEN

Preparing and Holding the Dissertation Defense

You should now be ready to get the dissertation into final shape. This chapter explains how to plan and prepare for your defense as well as what is needed to officially close your study.

PLANNING

The planning phase of the final dissertation defense is an exciting time. Taking the time to plan carefully and consider the components in Exhibit 19.1 will assist you in making this phase a success.

SECURE NEEDED RESOURCES

To begin the preparation process, you will need to secure three useful resources:

- The style guide you have been using
- Your university's guidelines for the preparation of theses and dissertations
- *How to Prepare Your Manuscript for Publication,* published by UMI Dissertation Services (300 North Zeeb Road, P.O. Box 1346, Ann Arbor, MI 48106)

The discussion that follows relies on the *Publication Manual of the American Psychological Association* and the UMI publication. As indicated previously, you should be using the style guide your chair recommends. Also note that the UMI publication indicates that the university's guidelines take precedence over UMI's.

Exhibit 19.1   Final Phase Dissertation Checklist

1. Secure needed resources

2. Edit the dissertation

3. Check on content and order

4. Write the abstract

5. Write the title and approval pages

6. Write the acknowledgments page

7. Write the table of contents and lists of tables and figures pages

8. Include the chapters

9. Finalize the references

10. Finalize any appendices

11. Submit dissertation to committee

EDIT THE DISSERTATION

You should use the aforementioned style guides to do your own editing first. Use the criteria specified in

Exhibit 19.2 to make your own corrections. Use the computer to check spelling, make more varied choices of words, and improve the style. Then read each chapter very carefully. Look for spelling errors that the spell checker might have missed. Reread Chapter 12 of this book, using the style reminders to correct any mistakes. Check all your tables and figures for accuracy and clarity.

Also keep in mind the preparation guidelines from UMI, as follows:

1. Use high-quality paper, minimum 20-pound weight, 8½ by 11 inches. Do not use erasable paper.

2. Double-space all text. Footnotes and extended quotations may be single-spaced.

3. Use a 10-point or 12-point font.

4. Use a letter quality printer.

5. Do not use correcting fluid or tape.

Most style manuals also recommend that you use a left margin of 1½ inches, to provide room for binding.

After you have done your own editing, have someone else use the same criteria in completing a second editing. Even though you consider yourself a good editor, you need an objective review by someone who is not so closely involved in the dissertation. Be sure to note that person's contribution in the "acknowledgments" section.

CHECK ON CONTENT AND ORDER

As part of the checking process, be sure you include all the elements in the order specified. Most dissertations include the following elements in the order specified here. Each of these is discussed in the sections that follow:

1. Abstract

2. Title page

3. Approval page

4. Acknowledgment page

5. Table of contents

6. List of tables and figures

7. Chapters of the dissertation

8. References

9. Appendices

Exhibit 19.2   Editing the Dissertation

DOES THE DISSERTATION . . .

Format

1. Follow the format specified by the university guidelines, the style manual, and the UMI publication (in that order of priority)?

Mechanics and Style

2. Use correct spelling and punctuation?

3. Use varied word choice?

4. Demonstrate a mature writing style, avoiding short simple sentences?

Content

5. Have a clear statement of the problem?

6. Explain clearly and completely the methodology?

7. Present the results accurately and clearly?

8. Summarize accurately and objectively the results of the study?

9. Discuss and interpret the results?

10. Make a significant contribution to the knowledge base?

Some universities specify a different order; be sure to check with the graduate school office or your chair.

WRITE THE ABSTRACT

The abstract is a summary of your dissertation. You should state the problem and briefly indicate the methodology. You also should summarize the results. Finally, briefly discuss the results.

In writing the abstract, ask yourself this question: "If I were a researcher trying to decide if this dissertation is worth retrieving, what would I want to know?" Remember that UMI limits abstracts to 350 words. **Do not include any bibliographic references, tables, figures, abbreviations, or acronyms.**

WRITE THE TITLE AND APPROVAL PAGES

Some universities require separate title and approval pages; some require one page that serves both functions. Check with your chair or graduate office. In choosing a title for your dissertation, keep in mind the needs of other researchers as they do a literature search. Keep the title as brief as possible and be sure it uses terms that will simplify retrieval. Do not use the words *study of* or similar terms. Here are some examples of poor and good titles.

POOR: A Study of Charter School Teachers and Their Motivation to Teach in Charter Schools

BETTER: Charter School Teachers: Reasons for Choosing Charter Schools

POOR: Research Into the Characteristics of Alternatively Certified Teachers Compared With Teachers Who Were Prepared in Traditional Programs

BETTER: Alternatively Certified Teachers and Traditionally Certified Teachers: Their Distinguishing Characteristics

WRITE THE ACKNOWLEDGMENT PAGE

The acknowledgment page is where you acknowledge all the help you have received. Typically, the acknowledgments include thanking the following: the chair, the other committee members, the editor, any funding source, the participants, family, and others. Do not try to be cute or effusive in your thanks. Also, be sure the chair approves this section; some chairs report that they are embarrassed by acknowledgments that are too effusive.

WRITE THE TABLE OF CONTENTS AND LISTS OF TABLES AND FIGURES

Most chairs prefer that you use the heading Contents for your table of contents. They do not want you to use this heading: Table of Contents. It is a table of contents, but the words *Table of* are not used in the heading. The same injunction applies to the lists of tables and figures. Use the headings Tables and Figures, unless your chair wants you to include the term *List of.*

INCLUDE THE CHAPTERS

Then assemble the chapters in order, checking to be sure that the pagination is correct. Also check with your chair about the style for the chapter heading. Here is the style usually preferred: "1. Introduction to the Study." The word *Chapter* is not included, and there is no underlining. In the terms used by the *Publication Manual* of the APA, the chapter title is a Level 1 heading.

FINALIZE THE REFERENCES

The list of references is a crucial part of the dissertation. It requires especially close checking. Here are some guidelines to follow. First, use the heading References. Do not use the words *List of* or call it *Bibliography*.

Also, be sure that you have included all the works—and only those works—cited in the text. Here is a simple way of checking. Separate the reference pages from the body of the dissertation; then read each chapter. As you find a reference, check it against the reference list. Are the names spelled correctly and listed in the proper order? In cases of multiple authorship, are the names listed in the same order? Is the date of publication correct? Has the style manual been followed scrupulously? Do all elements of the reference agree? Put a pencil mark next to each one that corresponds. The pencil marks will enable you to identify references that appear in the text but not in the reference list—and items that appear in the reference list but do not appear in the text.

FINALIZE ANY APPENDICES

Remember that appendices include materials that are better not included in the body of the text. Typically an appendix includes the following: a large table, a list of terms, samples of instruments, computer programs, and letters of permission or access. A special note about permissions is required here. You should get permission to reproduce any published tables or figures. Also, if you use a long quotation, you should check with the copyright holder to determine if permission is needed and will be given. Publications vary in their requirements here.

SUBMIT THE DISSERTATION

Now you are ready to submit the final dissertation to your chair, the other committee members, and your respective department (if required by your institution). When you have also held a successful defense, you will submit it to the graduate school office and to UMI Dissertation Services. UMI will submit your dissertation to the Copyright Office if you wish and will also make it available to other researchers upon request. You should find their manual, *Publishing Your Dissertation*, a very useful and detailed guide.

HOLDING THE DEFENSE

Your dissertation is ready. Now you face only the defense. How do you prepare yourself for it and conduct yourself during the hearing? These are the questions addressed here.

The answers will, of course, be somewhat influenced by the policies and procedures of your school. The following discussion reflects those in operation at many graduate schools, but you should be sure to determine how hearings are conducted at your school. If possible, attend other dissertation defenses and check with your chair about such matters as these: How long will the hearing last? What kind of initial presentation should you make? What role will your chair play? Should you or the chair take detailed notes during the hearing? Will you be able to use technological aids in making your presentation? How will the final results be determined?

Prepare

The first suggestion in preparing for the defense is to be sure that you have prepared and distributed to your committee the best possible copy of your dissertation. Procedures will vary here, depending on your chair's preferences and your school's requirements, but in general it makes sense to have an excellent draft prepared for the hearing. Even though you will probably have to make changes after the hearing, the good copy will make a more positive impact on the committee. A manuscript replete with errors and strikeovers invites criticism. Arrange matters so that the committee receives the copy two to three weeks prior to the hearing.

Next, review your dissertation until you know it backward and forward. Know all the major sources you have consulted. Be prepared to explain and defend your methodology. Know what your data mean; be prepared to interpret any tables or figures you have included. Know your last chapter so well that you can almost recite it by heart.

Listed in Exhibit 19.3 are the kinds of questions you can expect. Think about them in reference to your own dissertation and rehearse the answer you think you might give.

Finally, put yourself in the right frame of mind. You have done your best. If your chair has done his or her work and if you are able to conduct yourself reasonably well in the hearing, then you know you will pass—and you also know that you will probably be asked to make revisions. Panic and frantic anxiety will not help at this stage, so the night before the hearing, relax, rest, and do what else seems appropriate to help you feel at ease in the morning.

Ordinarily when all have assembled, the chair will ask you to leave. While you pace the floor outside, the chair is reviewing with the committee the procedures that will be followed. The chair is also using the time to smooth the way for you, since in many ways the chair is also on the spot. You then are summoned to return and the hearing begins.

Facilities

Arrive at the defense about 30 minutes ahead of time. If it seems appropriate to your chair, arrange to have coffee and pastries available for the committee. Check out the room, find out where you will be sitting, and check all other final arrangements. Greet faculty as they arrive; introduce any who might not know each other. Act as if it is your show and you know how to handle things.

Exhibit 19.3 Questions Typically Asked at Defense

1. Why did you choose that particular problem? Why did you not study this other problem instead?

2. What exactly were you trying to find out? I'm unclear about the meaning of your problem statement.

3. You have reviewed the important literature, but I fail to see what use you make of your review. Can you clarify for me what you learned from the review of the literature?

4. When you reviewed the literature, why did you decide to review that particular area of study?

5. Your review of the literature seems to omit these important contributions. Can you explain why these works and their findings do not appear in your review?

6. Your review of the literature includes this particular work, which is no longer considered a serious contribution. Why did you choose to include that work?

7. I think you may have misrepresented the findings of that study. Could you review for me what you think the study showed?

8. Why did you choose that particular method? Why did you not instead use this other method?

9. Can you clarify for me how the particular method you chose relates directly to the problem you chose to study?

10. What specifically was your relationship to the context and subjects of the study? Do you think that relationship in any way contaminated your study?

11. In what ways were that context or those subjects not representative? Have you been sensitive to that problem of atypicality?

12. Can you clarify for me what procedures you followed to ensure that your research observed the canons of the profession, with regard to ethical procedures?

13. I am unclear as to what that table means. Can you interpret it for me?

14. In the text of your dissertation you refer to this particular datum, but I cannot find any table or other support for that figure. Where does it come from?

15. The results you cite on this page seem somewhat in conflict with the results you cite elsewhere. Can you explain the discrepancy?

16. Can you account for this particular result, which seemingly would not have been predicted?

17. You posed certain specific questions in your first chapter. I am not clear that you answered each of those questions. Can you review those specific questions and relate them directly to your findings?

18. Your summary seems just a bit generally stated. Could you speak more specifically about your important findings?

19. I am not persuaded that your conclusions are supported by your findings. Could you explain to me specifically how this conclusion derives from the results of the study?

20. Your recommendations or your discussion of the implications of the study seem too sweeping to me. Can you explain specifically how you arrived at this particular recommendation?

21. If you had five minutes to speak to a group of colleagues about the implications of your study, what would you say?

22. If you were doing the study all over again, in what ways would you change it?

23. What are your plans for continuing your research in this area?

24. Can you relate your findings to other important research in the field? In what specific ways do you think you have made a contribution?

25. Your dissertation contains several proofreading errors. Were you aware of those errors?

Presentation

The defense usually begins with your chair asking you to present your study. Unless your chair advises you otherwise, act as if you are presenting a scholarly paper at a major conference. If possible, avoid using notes. Begin by explaining how and why you became interested in the problem. Discuss briefly the problem as you conceived it. Review your methodology. Focus mainly on the contents of your last chapter by summarizing, interpreting, and discussing your results.

Then the questioning will begin. This, of course, is the most crucial part. You want to respond in a way that suggests you are prepared to enter the community of scholars: You are informed, articulate, suitably humble in the presence of your elders, but quietly confident. Listen closely to each question. If you are unsure about what was asked, either paraphrase or ask for clarification. When you respond, avoid certain common errors that students typically make:

- Do not become defensive. If you are asked a question that seems to be a veiled attack, do not respond by counterattacking.
- Do not apologize or make excuses for yourself. If someone discovers a serious problem, listen, acknowledge the merits of the observation, and indicate that you appreciate the help.
- Do not blame your chair. It may well be that your chair gave you some bad advice, but the hearing is not the time to make that known. It is your dissertation; be responsible for it.
- Do not overstate your case or claim too much. Even if you have made a distinguished contribution to the field, let others say that.

AFTER YOUR PRESENTATION

At an appropriate time, your chair will ask you to leave the room while the committee discusses your defense and ballots on the final decision. When you have left, they will discuss the dissertation and your defense of it. If all is well, they will take only a few minutes to review the changes that must be made and to cast their votes. If there are problems with either the study or your defense, then they will need more time to decide among themselves what action should be taken.

At most universities, committees will make one of three decisions:

1. Dissertation is accepted.

2. Dissertation will be accepted, with minor changes made under the guidance of the chair.

3. Dissertation is not accepted; major changes are required, with final approval by the committee.

When the vote is in and you are told, probably, that you have "passed, with minor changes to be made," thank all participants and make arrangements at once to consult with your chair about the changes to be made and the final steps to be taken.

AFTER THE DEFENSE

Immediately following the defense, you should take the time to meet with your dissertation chair to debrief on the dissertation defense. This debriefing should include what went specifically well and what you would have done differently during the presentation. You should also discuss with your chair the remaining time line of tasks required to complete the dissertation submission process. Taking the time to review final processes will be of benefit to you in the days to come.

University Requirements

As discussed previously, specific university requirements need to be met to successfully complete the dissertation. You need to consider such items as graduation registration, regalia requirements, and diploma specifics.

Graduate School. Check again with the university graduate school to ascertain such things as due dates and submission protocols.

Completed Dissertation Submission. Each university has specific guidelines for dissertation submission. You are encouraged to remain up-to-date on such information so that the submission phase is completed by the university due date. Being unaware of these guidelines may impact your graduation and completion of the dissertation. Depending on the university guidelines, dissertations may be submitted via hard copy or electronically. In either case, knowing and following the specific guidelines is important to successfully completing the submission phase.

University Graduate School or University Library

Dissertations are commonly submitted simultaneously or consecutively to the university graduate school or university library. This process should be outlined within the graduate school submission processes and procedures.

Electronic

The electronic submission and storage of dissertations has become a popular practice among universities. This method decreases the amount of time, paper, and resources needed to manage dissertation submission and storage. The electronic method also allows for ease of access by others as well as the capacity to be viewed by a larger audience. Each university has protocols for electronic submission.

IRB COMPLETION REQUIREMENTS

It Is important to remember the completion requirements of the Institutional Review Board (IRB). Failure to submit the appropriate paperwork is negligent research practice.

Study Closure

Once you have completed your dissertation, obtained all necessary signatures, submitted your dissertation to the required offices noted by the university, and received notification that your study has been accepted and filed according to university guidelines, it is time to complete one final task—the IRB Closure Form. You may work with your chair to ensure the closure form is correctly completed and submitted.

The IRB Closure Form notifies the IRB office that you have concluded the research and no longer want to pursue the research associated with this study. Once the IRB Closure Form is submitted and that office has reviewed your request, you should receive notification that the study has been closed. If you do not receive such notification from the IRB office, you may want to contact them to ascertain the process of such notification.

Documentation

You need to maintain all documentation regarding correspondence with the IRB office. It is your professional responsibility to maintain this information in case the need arises for you to produce It. A good rule is to maintain documents such as this for a period of five years, at which point you may discard it or continue to store it in your professional files.

TECHNOLOGY TECHNIQUE: PACKAGING THE FINAL DRAFT OF THE DISSERTATION

Once you have completed the dissertation, how you store the information will be important because you will often want to reference your work. Storing the completed dissertation on three separate CDs is the safest method of ensuring future access. Additionally, when saving the dissertation to each CD, a good practice is to save each chapter and related section separately. This method will allow to you access parts of the study without having to access and scroll through the document just to read a specific section. For example, on each disk have a separate document file for the abstract, each chapter, the tables, figures, appendices, and references. You may also wants to do the same for the acknowledgments and any other component of the study.

TWENTY

Publishing From the Thesis or Dissertation

As soon as you have successfully defended your dissertation, you should consider publishing from it. Give serious consideration to publishing in one of these four venues: adding to the research knowledge base, presenting a scholarly paper at a conference, writing a journal article, or writing a book.

ADD TO THE RESEARCH KNOWLEDGE BASE

You should add to the knowledge base by sending your dissertation along with the abstract to two electronic knowledge bases. First, you should send the abstract and dissertation to the Education Resources Information Center (ERIC). You probably retrieved articles from ERIC as you developed your review of the literature. Now it is time for you to return the favor by making sure that what you learned is available to the profession. You can check with the reference specialist at your university library, or you can access ERIC at this Internet address: www.eric.edu.gov

You also should send a copy of your dissertation along with an abstract to UMI. Their very helpful guide for publishing your dissertation is titled *Publishing Your Dissertation: How to Prepare Your Manuscript for Publication*; it is available from UMI Dissertation Services, 300 North Zeeb Road, P.O. Box 1346, Ann Arbor, MI 48106. In preparing your materials for both groups, be sure to check with your graduate school, since schools vary in their requirements for submission.

PRESENT A SCHOLARLY PAPER

The second step is to present a paper at a scholarly conference. You should submit a proposal to one of the professional associations in your field. Each association, upon request, will send detailed guidelines about the forums available, the length of the presentation, and the nature of the proposal desired. Follow those instructions carefully in submitting a proposal based on your dissertation.

Presenting a paper at a scholarly conference has several advantages. The most important is that doing so will place you in a network of professionals with similar interests. They will learn from you and you from them. It is also a key step in advancing your career, especially if you plan a career in higher education. Finally, it is one major way of contributing to the knowledge base in your field. After presenting a paper at a major conference, you may receive a request from the ERIC staff asking you to submit your paper for inclusion in the ERIC database.

If your conference proposal is accepted, analyze the likely audience. Will most be practitioners or other researchers? The answer will influence how you organize and deliver your paper. Practitioners will expect an emphasis on the practical implications of your study; they will appreciate receiving handouts that they can carry back home.

Here is an outline for a 30-minute presentation to an audience of practitioners:

1. What you learned: two minutes (a very general statement as an introduction)

2. Your methodology: three minutes

3. A detailed summary of your results: five minutes

4. Applications for practice: 20 minutes

Researchers will be more interested in your methodology and the relationship of your research to the existing knowledge base. They will appreciate receiving a copy of the last chapter of your dissertation, formatted as a scholarly paper.

Here is an outline for a 30-minute presentation to a scholarly audience:

1. Problem statement: two minutes

2. Methodology: six minutes

3. Summary of results: seven minutes

4. Discussion, interpretation, and relationship to prior research: 15 minutes

Regardless of the audience, keep in mind some basic rules of presenting to a large group:

- Do not read to them. You may refer to notes or use a transparency to remind you and the audience of key points.
- Use effective visuals to supplement the oral presentation.
- Err on the side of brevity. Allow ample time for questions and discussion.

Publish a Journal Article

You should also use your dissertation research as the basis of a journal article. The following steps will help you get your article published.

Identify Several Possible Journals

The first step is to identify four or five journals to which you might submit your article. You should undertake a systematic study of these journals so that your article fits the journal. This step is a vital beginning step since journals vary in emphasis, audience, length of article, and style.

In analyzing the journal, you may find the form shown in Exhibit 20.1 helpful. The entries in the form will be explained briefly.

In addition to the journal itself, you should find these resources helpful:

- *Phi Delta Kappan* periodically publishes an article on writing for publication that contains very useful information on most of the educational journals. Check the most recent article.
- The Richardson and Prickett (1991) manual briefly describes several hundred journals in the field of education.
- *Ulrich's International Periodical Directory* and *Magazines for Librarians* are two references available at university libraries; they both provide useful information about most of the educational journals.
- Several recent issues of the journals you are considering will be useful in helping you analyze the audience, content, and style.

Make a Careful Analysis of Each Journal

Take each journal and make a systematic analysis, following these guidelines:

Exhibit 20.1 Analysis of Journal

Title: _____

Editor: _____

Address for submitting manuscripts: _____

_____

Frequency of publication: _____

Primary audience: _____

Style guide: _____

Theme issues and dates: _____

Length of articles: _____

Number of hard copies to be submitted: _____

Disk to be submitted? _____

Refereed? _____

Acceptance rate: _____

Decision time: _____

Is a query recommended? _____

Other guidelines: _____

Basic Information. Identify the title of the journal, the name of the editor, and the address for submitting manuscripts. Note that smaller journals with part-time editors will have one address for business matters and one address for submitting manuscripts.

Frequency of Publication. Note whether it publishes on a monthly, bimonthly, or irregular schedule. Several educational journals do not publish during the summer.

Primary Audience. This is a key piece of information. The primary audience is most of the readers who subscribe to the journal. Here are some primary audiences, just as examples: school administrators, classroom teachers, school librarians, and university professors and researchers. The primary audience will affect the organization, content, and style of your article.

Style Guide. Each journal has its own style guide, differing chiefly in how references are handled. Some journals use footnotes, some use endnotes, and some use citations in text (the method used in this book). You should scrupulously follow the style guide recommended.

Theme Issues and Dates. Some journals identify a theme for a particular year. For example, the *Delta Pi Epsilon Journal* is planning a themed special edition concerning "Social Media" (http://www.dpe.org/DPE_Journal_Social_Media_Call_for_Papers_2012.pdf). If you submit an article related to the specified theme, your article will have a better chance of being accepted.

Submission Specifications. Note the length of articles published in the journal, the number of hard copies to be submitted, and whether a disk is required (and the recommended word processing software).

Use of Referees. Scholarly journals send articles submitted to respected authorities in the field who are called *referees.* These authorities evaluate the article and submit their recommendations to the editor. This information is useful for three reasons. First, refereed journals are much more selective; your chances of being published are therefore limited. Also, if you aspire to a career in higher education, selection committees look closely at your list of publications to determine whether your articles were published in refereed or nonrefereed journals. Finally, the editors of refereed journals are slower in their response time, since they must wait for the reports of referees.

Acceptance Rate. The acceptance rate is the percentage of articles published, based on the number submitted. Very selective journals might have an acceptance rate as low as 10 percent; less selective journals may publish as many as 80 percent of the articles submitted. In general, you should submit your first article to a journal with a moderately high acceptance rate, unless you believe that your research is so important that you wish to be published in a journal that is highly selective.

Decision Time. Note the time typically required for the editor to make a decision to publish your article. If your article is clearly unfit for that journal, you will usually hear in a few weeks. Most editors will decide in a month or two, but in some cases you may have to wait as long as six to eight months.

Query Recommended. Some journals prefer that you submit a query letter before submitting an article. A query letter briefly describes the article and outlines its contents. Other editors do not wish to receive a query letter; they want to review the article itself as the first step.

Prepare the Article for Submission

Once you have analyzed and identified a few journals that might publish your article, select the one that seems best. Write your article to meet its specifications. In doing so, you should, of course, draw upon your research. However, if you are writing for practitioners, do not follow the organization of the dissertation. Emphasize your summary and discussion, focusing chiefly on its applications for practice.

When you have written your first draft, ask two or three colleagues to critique your article before submitting it. Make the revisions they suggest. Make four copies of the final version—one for you and three for the editor of the journal. Then send the three copies to the editor of the journal, with a very brief cover letter. Indicate that you do not wish to have the copies returned if the article is not selected for publication, unless the journal requires you to send a self-addressed stamped envelope. Wait patiently. Do not bother the editor with telephone calls or written reminders. Remember that it may take the editor several months to decide.

Do not submit the same article to more than one journal at a time. If your first journal rejects it, revise it again and submit it to your second choice.

DEVELOP A PLAN TO PUBLISH A BOOK

You also should consider using your dissertation research as the basis for a book you might write. You will have to do considerable work to move from dissertation to book, but the benefits derived are worth the work expended.

The process of developing a plan to publish a book is somewhat similar to that for submitting an article. Begin by identifying and securing copies of from four to six major books in the field in which you hope to publish. Note the publishers of those books, because you probably should *not* submit your plan to them. Most publishers do not wish to publish books that will compete with books on their active list. Next identify three or four other publishers who publish in that general field but seem not to have published similar works.

Once you have identified some possible publishers, develop a *book plan.* (Some publishers call this proposal a *prospectus.*) The book plan is a proposal you will submit to the publisher to assist the editors in determining if they even wish to consider publishing your book. The typical contents of a book plan are shown in Exhibit 20.2; the major components will be explained briefly here.

Exhibit 20.2 Book Plan

1. Author: (Résumé attached) _____
2. Working title _____
3. Brief description of book _____
4. Primary audience _____
5. Secondary audiences _____
6. Approximate number of manuscript pages _____
7. Date for submission of manuscript _____
8. Analysis of competition _____
9. Table of contents (attached) _____
10. Sample chapter (enclosed) _____

Complete the Book Plan

The following components should be included in your book plan.

Author and Working Title. Note your name and enclose your résumé. The *working title* is your tentative title. If your plan is accepted, the publisher will consult with you about the final title, weighing marketing factors.

Brief Description of the Book. Describe the book in 50 to 100 words. Explain the purpose of the work and its general content.

Audiences. The primary audience consists of the readers to whom the book will be marketed. The secondary audiences are others who might read the book. For example, the primary audience for this book is graduate students writing a thesis or a dissertation; the secondary audience is the faculty who advise them.

Book Length. Estimate the number of manuscript pages; the publisher can then translate that figure into the number of printed pages.

Submission Date. Usually you will be wiser to indicate the number of months after contracts have been signed.

Analysis of Competition. This is perhaps the most critical component of the book plan. The publisher wants you to answer this question: "How do we know that the proposed book will sell?" To answer this question, you should develop a form similar to the one shown in Exhibit 20.3. (Exhibit 20.3 shows only part of the form.) The completed form will show at a glance how your proposed work compares with the major competing works. When you have completed that form, you can then comment briefly on the highlights.

Table of Contents. Attach on a separate page a detailed table of contents. Do not list only chapter titles; indicate the major sections of each chapter.

Sample Chapter. Usually the editors will want to see a sample chapter, as a way of assessing your writing ability.

Exhibit 20.3 Analysis of Competition

	This Book	*Book 1*	*Book 2*	*Book 3*
Understanding the context for charter schools	x		x	
Organizing your constituents	x	x		x
Developing the charter	x	Very brief treatment		x
Selecting the staff	x		x	x

Submit the Book Plan

Ask a colleague to review your book plan. Then select the publisher most likely to publish the book. Do not send it to more than one publisher at a time. Enclose a brief cover letter, addressed to the acquisitions editor.

Technology Technique: Journal Software Requirements

Journal Software Requirements. The software requirements for journals have fairly consistent guidelines. View the appropriate journal's website for specific information to ensure compatibility.

Submission Requirements. Once you have determined the journal to which you will submit your manuscript, take the time to review their submission requirements. These requirements vary somewhat from journal to journal; however, there are several consistent themes found in each: for example, the size of font, margins, the removal of author identification for blind review process, and font style. Following the correct submission requirements is the first step toward having your work accepted for publication.

Word Count. The word count feature, as mentioned in a previous chapter, is a function that may be used to help you determine the length of the submission requirements. Often, abstracts, biographies, and length of manuscript have a required minimum and/or maximum word count. The utilization of this function will save you time and energy as you are able to quickly add or delete text to meet the submission guidelines.

References

American Psychological Association. (1990). Ethical principles of psychologists: Amended June 2, 1989. *American Psychologist, 57,* 390–395.

American Psychological Association. (2002). Ethical principles of psychologists and code of conduct. *American Psychologist, 57,* 1060–1073.

American Psychological Association. (2010). *Publication manual of the American Psychological Association* (6th ed.). Washington, DC: Author.

Apple, M. W. (Ed.). (1997). *Review of research in education* (Vol. 22). Washington, DC: American Educational Research Association.

Cochran, W. (1977). *Sampling techniques* (3rd ed.). New York, NY: John Wiley.

Cohen, L., Manion, L., & Morrison, K. (2007). *Research methods in education* (6th ed.). Milton Park, Abingdon, Oxon, UK: Routledge.

Council of Graduate Schools. (1991). *The role and nature of the doctoral dissertation.* Washington, DC: Author.

CPED: The Carnegie Project on the Education Doctorate—An inter-institutional discussion about reclaiming the education doctorate. (2012). About the study. Retrieved from http://cpedinitiative.org/about-study

Creswell, J. W. (2009). *Research design: Qualitative, quantitative, and mixed method approaches* (6th ed.). Thousand Oaks, CA: Sage.

D'Andrea, L. M. (1997). *Obstacles to completing a doctoral program.* Unpublished manuscript, University of Nevada Reno.

D'Belcher, A. H. (2005). Writing the qualitative dissertation: What motivates and sustains commitment to a fuzzy genre? *Journal of English for Academic Purposes, 4*(3), 187–205.

Electronic note card. (n.d.). Retrieved from http://webcache.googleusercontent.com/search?q=cache:fziklUjKrQYJ:drb.lifestreamcenter.net/E-note.rtf+electronic+note+cards&cd=1&hl=en&ct=clnk&gl=us

Flood, J., Jensen, J. M., Lapp, D., & Squire, J. R. (Eds.). (1991). *Handbook of research on teaching the English language arts.* New York, NY: Macmillan.

Germeroth, D. (1990, November). *Lonely days and lonely nights: Completing the doctoral dissertation.* Paper presented at the annual meeting of the Speech Communication Association, Chicago.

Hoy, W. K., & Miskel, C. G. (1987). *Educational administration: Theory, research, and practice* (3rd ed.). New York, NY: Random House.

Hubbard, R. S., & Power, B. M. (2003). *The art of classroom inquiry.* Portsmouth, NH: Heinemann.

Huberman, M., & Miles, M. B. (Eds.). (2002). *The qualitative researcher's companion.* Thousand Oaks, CA: Sage.

Huck, S. W. (2012). *Reading statistics and research* (6th ed.). Saddle River, NJ: Pearson Education.

Huguley, S. (1989). An investigation of obstacles to completion of the dissertation and of doctoral student attitudes toward the dissertation experience. *Dissertation Abstracts International, 50,* 372-A.

Janis, I. L., & Mann, L. (1977). *Decision making: A psychological analysis of conflict, choice, and commitment.* New York, NY: Free Press.

Kaplowitz, M. D., Hadlock, T. D., & Levine, R. (2004). A comparison of web and mail survey response rates. *Public Opinion Quarterly, 68*(1), 94–101.

Kline, D. (n.d.). Writer's guide for R&D proposals. Retrieved from http://education.astate.edu/dcline/guide/Limitations.html

McMillan, J. H. (2012). *Educational research: Fundamentals for the consumer* (6th ed.). Boston, MA: Pearson.

Melroy, J. M. (1994). *Writing the qualitative dissertation.* Hillsdale, NJ: Lawrence Erlbaum.

Melroy, J. M. (2002). *Writing the qualitative dissertation* (2nd ed.). Mahwah, NJ: Lawrence Erlbaum.

Merriam, S. B. (2001). *Qualitative research and case study research in education.* San Francisco, CA: Jossey-Bass.

Morgan, D. L. (1997). *Practical strategies for combining qualitative and quantitative methods.* Portland, OR: Portland State University Press.

National Council of Professors of Educational Administration. (2011, February 4). *The handbook of doctoral programs: Issues and challenges.* Connexions. Houston, TX: Rice University.

Northern Illinois University Counseling and Student Development Center. (2012). *Coaching for academic success: Obstacles to completing theses and dissertations.* Retrieved from http://www.niu.edu/csdc/coaching/theses_dissertations.shtml

Parson, A. (2012). System requirements for Skype. SALON Media Group. Retrieved from http://techtips.salon.com/system-requirements-skype-4185.html

Richardson, M. D., & Prickett, R. L. (1991). *Publication sources in educational leadership.* Lancaster, PA: Technomic.

Schensul, J. J., & LeCompte, M. D. (Eds.). (1999). *Theethnographer's toolkit.* Walnut Creek, CA: AltaMira Press.

Tadeusik, C. J. (1989). *Stress and coping among first year doctoral students. Dissertation Abstracts International, 49,* 3670-A.

UMI Dissertation Services. (2003). *Publishing your dissertation: How to prepare your manuscript for publication.* Ann Arbor, MI: Author.

Wehmeyer, L. B. (1995). *The educator's information highway.* Lancaster, PA: Technomic.

Whitted, J. (1987). Ph.D. candidates' stresses and strains related to their dissertation process. *Dissertation Abstracts International, 48,* 1402-A.

Writing Center at the University of North Carolina at Chapel Hill. (2012). *Dissertations.* Retrieved from http://writingcen ter.unc.edu/resources/handouts-demos/specific-writing-assignments/dissertations

Yin, R. K. (2009). *Case study research: Design and methods.* Thousand Oaks, CA: Sage.

Index

Pages followed by e indicate exhibits